MW01142386

THE
GROWING-OLDER
GUIDE TO
REAL ESTATE

What Everyone Over Fifty Should Know About
Buying, Selling, Financing and Owning a Home

by
H. L. Kibbey

Panoply Press, Incorporated
Lake Oswego, Oregon

Cover design: Bruce DeRoos
Cover art: Krieg Barrie
Illustrations: Janora Bayot

Printed in the United States of America.

 Text has been printed on recycled paper.

Library of Congress Cataloging-in-Publication Data
Kibbey, H. L.,
        The growing-older guide to real estate : what everyone
over 50 should know about buying, selling, financing, and
owning a home / H. L. Kibbey
            p. cm.
        Includes index.
        ISBN 0-9615067-8-4
        1. Real estate investment - -United States. 2.. Aged - -
United States- -Dwellings. 3. Housing - -United States - -
Finance. I. Title.
HD255.K5 1993
332.63'24 - -dc20   93-20383
                                                                              CIP

Published by:
Panoply Press, Inc.
P.O. Box 1885
Lake Oswego, Oregon 97035
(503) 697-7964

Publisher's catalog is available upon request.

Acknowledgments

This book has been a pleasure to write, thanks to the help of so many friends, advisors and associates, among them: Byron Kibbey, Diane Gronholm, KiKi Canniff, Colleen J. Watkins, Ruth Klein, Susan Weber, Robert McSweeny JD, Neil Farmer C.F.R.E., Darlene Hess and John F. Scott. And to the talented cover designer and illustrators: Bruce DeRoos, Janora Bayot and Krieg Barrie, all I can say is, "Great job!"

Any real estate decision should be researched thoroughly; mistakes can be costly in terms of both your bank account and peace of mind. Learn to rely on a team of qualified professional advisors- -your accountant, attorney, real estate agent and loan officer- -to give you the help you need. The information in this book, while carefully compiled, is not intended to be used as a substitute for competent professional financial and legal advice. Remember, too, that financing facts and figures are subject to change.

To Bob and Ruth Kibbey...

who have been a treasured source of encouragement and
inspiration to me
for many, many years.

TABLE OF CONTENTS

Part VI. A FINAL WORD

Part I
CHOICES

1

Real Estate Concerns for Those over Fifty

Most real estate books are written for the young. Whether they openly admit to this fact or not, the evidence speaks for itself. You'll find hundreds of books on the market today which adequately address the needs of the first-time buyer, the move-up buyer, the seller and the investor. I know, because I've contributed my share of titles to the wealth of literature on the subject.

But what about the over-fifty generation? Although some of their real estate questions and problems are similar to those of younger homeowners, they have, in addition, another set of concerns common to many older Americans. Most books for homebuyers and sellers do a poor job in addressing their particular requirements. The advice that works well for a young family trading up to a larger home has little relevance to older couples looking at smaller homes for retirement or wondering how to get their hands on the equity tied up in their present home. Trying to adapt a generic real estate book to the specific needs and problems of this age group is a little like trying to stuff sixty-five-year-old feet into a pair of roller blades. It works for a few, but is downright foolhardly for most.

That is why I've written this book. If you're over fifty, if you have parents in that age bracket, or if you're close enough to that magic number to be thinking about life thereafter, this book is especially for you. Whether you own a home now and are considering selling, refinancing or donating it to a non-profit organization, whether you are contemplating the purchase of a retirement home or are planning to go on living in your present home, you'll find valuable information in these pages.

Perhaps your main real estate concern is simply holding onto your present home, in the face of fixed or diminishing income and rising ownership expenses. If so, take heart; there are ways to ease the financial crunch that may allow you to continue to live in your home for many more years. And finally, if the IRS rules and regulations concerning capital gains and other ownership matters have you wondering what your next move should be, this book will help you resolve those questions and prepare a well-organized plan for the real estate in your life.

2

Making Decisions

As you grow older and approach or reach retirement age, your housing needs change. Children grow up and leave home, long-term mortgages may by now be paid off, ties to the community you've lived and worked in may seem less binding. Change is often a factor in later-life real estate ventures, and with change comes the need to make decisions. You may decide to sell your home and buy a retirement home elsewhere, or you may decide to stay where you are and adapt your present home physically (and financially) to meet your needs. As you age, tax issues relating to real estate matters increase in importance and complexity.

All of these are concerns that will affect you after the age of fifty. It is my intent, in this book, to cover the real estate decisions that you as an older American may be called upon to make, with respect to the homes that you own now or will buy for retirement. You'll find included here valuable information about acquiring, selling, financing, holding onto or giving your home to charity, and help in making the decisions behind those transactions.

There's been plenty of over-fifty real estate activity going on in my own family lately, with two sets of aunts and uncles (in their seventies and eighties) buying and selling property to meet their retirement needs. On the whole, the various transactions were successful in that they were "quick and clean". But in at least one case, the participants were left with a feeling of dissatisfaction over the outcome. Had they made the best possible decision? Did they list their home at a high enough price? Did they accept the first offer too quickly? Who would have thought that closing costs and tax on their capital gain would reduce their proceeds by this much? Would they have been better off holding onto their home and renting it? Doubts about the wisdom of their sale may continue to worry them for months or years to come. But it doesn't have to be this way.

Real estate decisions are often highly charged with emotion. I'm afraid it just goes with the territory, especially when your own home is at stake. We're all subject to this affliction to one degree or another. At a time when we need to make a level-headed business decision about our home, emotions cloud our thinking and doubts creep in. However the best way to arm yourself against the emotional turmoil of housing decisions is to learn as much as you can about the real estate market, financing techniques and settlement procedures before you even consider your plan of action. Your decisions will then be backed up by a thorough knowledge of the rules of the game and you'll find yourself dealing with wisdom rather than emotion.

Guidelines for a Successful Transaction

Here are points to consider before you buy or sell a home:

- Recognize that real estate markets and financing techniques change rapidly. How long has it been since you bought, sold or financed a home? Unless you have been actively involved in the real estate market in your community within the last year or two, what you've learned from past dealings may not necessarily apply in today's transactions.

- Take plenty of time to make a decision about your home. Do not rush a real estate matter. Assemble all the facts you'll need to make an informed decision, double check them for accuracy, then sleep on it.

- Do not be fooled into thinking that there is a "window of opportunity" for buying or selling your home, one that you may miss unless you act quickly. That kind of panic-driven action causes even the most normally clear-headed individuals to make expensive mistakes.

- Accept real estate advice only from those who are qualified to give it. So your neighbor tells you the market is "hot" and thinks you'll easily get $195,000 for your home? Don't listen, unless your neighbor happens to be a licensed residential real estate appraiser who has spent time inspecting, measuring, and evaluating your home while preparing a written appraisal.

- Which brings me to my next point: Never accept an opinion of value without hard facts to back it up.

- Don't place your real estate transaction entirely in the hands of your real estate agent. Take time to be knowledgeable about the housing market and real estate practices so that you can make decisions confidently.

- Assemble a team of qualified professionals: a real estate agent, attorney, accountant and loan officer.

- In short, be knowledgeable, be aware and be in control of your real estate decisions.

Part II
CASH IN
AND STAY PUT

Part II
CASH IN
AND STAY PUT

There are many reasons older Americans feel the desire to pull up roots and opt for a change of address. Weather may be better in another state, offspring and grandchildren who have settled elsewhere may be a strong magnetic force, and lifestyle changes are often especially enticing to those who now have the time to enjoy them.

Then there are also compelling financial reasons to move. The home you presently own may be far too expensive to maintain, now that you're facing retirement. Property taxes and maintenance don't retire with you, they keep clamoring to be paid. If you've owned your home for many years, bought it with cash, or paid off a mortgage loan, you may find yourself living in a veritable goldmine. Property values have appreciated as your funds have been poured down the shaft each month. The value of your investment is there all right, but of what earthly use is a goldmine if you aren't equipped with heavy-duty mining equipment to claim the wealth that is yours?

Before you decide that your only option is to sell your home, in order to afford to live comfortably or to have money to spend on other things, read the following chapters carefully. In this section of the book, we'll take a look at other choices open to you, ways to extract money from that goldmine, so that your house helps to pay its own way.

3

Convert Your Home Equity into Cash

EQUITY is the amount equal to the value of your home minus the total amount of any loans against it.

Homes can have an insatiable appetite for cash. With long years of mortgage payments and money spent on maintenance and improvements, year in and year out, you've no doubt invested an astonishing amount in your house by retirement time. But look at the brighter side for a moment. If you've owned your home for several years, no doubt you've acquired considerable **equity** by paying off your mortgage loans and improving the property. Your equity has grown even larger as the value of your home has increased through inflation.

So here you are, with a valuable asset that's worth appreciably more than you paid for it. But it (and you) continue to need cash. You and the mortgage may have retired but the tax assessor hasn't and the upkeep is as demanding as ever. Sometimes it seems that your cash is locked up tighter than Fort Knox. All of a sudden the thought hits home: real estate is not a particularly liquid investment. It's not like a savings account; you can't immediately withdraw your invested money when you need it. So how can you get your hands on it?

Selling your home is one solution, of course, but often not an immediate one and perhaps not an appealing one. It takes time to put a home on the market, attract a willing and able buyer, then wait for the appraisal, loan approval and settlement. Besides that, you may simply prefer to go on living right where you are.

Cash is often at the root of the problem: your present income may be insufficient to maintain you and your home, or you may be wishing you had some of that money your home so willingly ate, to travel or pay other debts. If it's cash you need, then maybe it's time your home came to your rescue. You "fed" it and cared for it all these years, now let's see what it can do for you!

There are several possible ways to cash in the equity that's been building in your home over the years. Starting in this chapter, we'll look at the commonly used methods: refinances, equity loans, reverse annuity mortgages, and, of course, the sale of your home, with variations on this theme that permit you to remain living in it, if that is your choice. These methods are alike in only one respect: they enable the homeowner to convert that valuable equity into cash. But they accomplish this goal in very different ways, as you'll discover in the following pages. If you're a homeowner with substantial equity in your home, one of these techniques may help you tap into it.

EQUITY VALUE WORKSHEET

Here's how to calculate the value of your equity:

A. Current balance of your 1st mortgage loan: _____

B. Current balance of your 2nd mortgage loan: _____

C. Total amount of any other loans secured by your home (such as a home improvement loan): _____

D. Other debts or incumbrances against your home (such as tax liens or deferred property tax) _____

E. Add together items A+B+C+D: _____

F. Realistic market value of your home today: _____

Minus your answer to item E: _____

The value of the equity in your home: _____

The table on the following pages illustrates other differences in the plans themselves and in the needs that they meet:

Convert Your Home
Which method would

	Retain ownership of home	Live in home indefinitely	May be required to move at some time	Must vacate home	Borrower must make payments	No repayment while living in home	Interest charged	Fees or closing costs charged	Lien placed on home
Refinance	✔	✔			✔		✔	✔	✔
Equity Loan	✔	✔			✔		✔	✔	✔
RAM (insured)	✔	✔				✔	✔	✔	✔
RAM (uninsured)	✔		✘			✔	✔	✔	✔
Deferred Loans	✔	✔				✔	✘		✔
Property Tax Deferral	✔	✔				✔	✔		✔
Sale				✔				✘✘	
Sale w/ Leaseback		✘	✘					✘✘	
Sale w/ Life Estate	●●	✔						✘✘	

✘   Depends upon particular terms of agreement or program selected.

✘✘   Negotiable. Some of seller's closing costs may be paid by buyer.

Equity Into Cash
best meet your needs?

Owner pays for insurance & upkeep	Receive lump sum in cash	Owner may receive monthly income	Cash withdrawals as needed	Cash proceeds may be used for designated purpose	Must have sufficient income to qualify	Low to moderate income limits	Minimum age requirement	Home must be owned free & clear, or nearly so	
✓	✓				✓				**Refinance**
✓	✓	✓			✓				**Equity Loan**
✓	✓	✓	✓				✓	✓	**RAM (insured)**
✓	✓	✓	✓				✓	✓	**RAM (uninsured)**
✓	✓			✓		✗	✗	✗	**Deferred Loans**
✓	✗			✓		✗	✗		**Property Tax Deferral**
	✓	✗							**Sale**
✓	✓	✓							**Sale w/ Leaseback**
●●	✓								**Sale w/ Life Estate**

● Owner of life estate pays upkeep.
●● Retains ownership of life estate.

How Much Cash Can You Expect to Receive?

In any of the methods of equity conversion outlined in this book, there are limits to the amount of equity that can be converted to cash. It is unlikely that you will be able to receive cash for the entire amount of equity in your calculations, or even come close. For example, most lenders follow fairly rigid guidelines in determining maximum loan amounts. Even if you sell your home (the ultimate conversion method, since you'll technically be cashing in 100% of your equity in most cases), your estimated proceeds will be reduced by closing costs, real estate commission and possibly the tax on your capital gain. So it is important to evaluate the various methods carefully with this in mind.

4

Refinances

REFINANCING is the process of obtaining a new loan for your existing home. This "refi" will replace any mortgage loans you currently owe and may provide additional cash.

There are two main reasons homeowners choose to refinance a home: first, to replace an existing loan that is not as attractive as it might be. (For example, it may be a loan at a much higher interest rate than is available today, or perhaps it's an adjustable-rate, rather than a fixed-rate loan.)

The second reason to refinance is to obtain cash for some of the equity that has built up in your home over the years. You'll notice that I used the word 'some' in the last sentence. Do not expect to be able to cash out your entire equity; lending rules customarily do not permit refinance loans up to 100% of the home's value, especially when the homeowner will receive cash.

Refinancing Can Be Expensive

Be cautious about refinancing your home. "Refis" are expensive; the loan fees and closing costs are similar to those charged by a lender for a loan to purchase a home and usually total thousands of dollars. (See the closing costs table in chapter 14.) You'll still need to pay for an appraisal and credit report, plus loan fees and perhaps discount points, mortgage insurance (if required), title insurance for the lender, escrow and recording fees. You will not necessarily need to have this amount in cash; on many refinances, the homeowner is permitted to finance the closing costs and loan fees by adding them to the loan amount. The deciding factors will be the amount of equity you have in your home and the size of loan you are requesting.

How Large a Loan Can You Get?

If you are simply replacing an unattractive existing loan and do not need or want to receive additional cash, your lender may allow you to refinance up to 90% of the value of your home. (On a $100,000 home, for example, you'd be able to replace a loan up to $90,000.) However, if you want to receive cash out of the transaction, over and above your existing loan amount, you will usually be limited to about 75% of the home's appraised value. (For example, on a $100,000 home with a $50,000 existing loan to be paid off at closing, you could receive up to a $75,000 loan, with $25,000 cash, less your closing costs.)

Refinancing a Second Home

If you're trying to refinance a second home or vacation home (a home that is not your primary residence), you'll find more stringent rules: lenders will usually finance up to 70% of the home's value when an existing loan is simply being replaced. "Cash out" is rarely permitted for second home financing— an important point to consider if you're thinking of buying a vacation home as an investment. It is often more difficult to extract cash from a home that is not your primary residence.

Replacing an Existing Loan

When does it make sense to replace your existing financing with a 'better' loan? Here's the rule of thumb: If you can reduce your interest rate by at least 2% or if you can 'improve' the type of loan (moving from a high interest adjustable-rate loan to a fixed-rate loan, for example), consider a refinance. The 2% rule isn't hard and fast, but if you plan to stay in your home only a few more years, you may not recoup the cost of a refinance if the difference is much less than that. Ask a loan officer to give you a detailed estimate of all likely loan fees and closing costs before you make a decision.

Tax Tip for Refinances

If you decide to refinance, be aware of this tax rule: Discount points paid on a refinance are not fully deductible that year, with the exception of those paid on funds that are spent on improvements to your home.

Qualifying for a Refinance

The qualifying guidelines for refinances are the same as for those of a purchase money loan (refer to chapter 14). Your creditworthiness will be evaluated on three factors: your income and assets, your debts and liabilities, and your recent credit history. Age is not a consideration here. You cannot be denied a 30-year loan simply because you are 57, 77 or 97 years old.

Where to Obtain a Loan

If you were pleased with the service you received from the lending institution that financed your home previously, then make an appointment there to inquire about refinancing your home. It is possible that your former lender may offer you a slightly reduced interest rate or loan fee for returning on a refinance, but don't expect it. Usually the concession, if one is offered at all, is so slight that it should not be a deciding factor in your choice of lender.

On a refinance, it is wise to do just as much comparison-shopping among lenders as you would for a first-time loan. So I hope that you will take time to study the financing information in chapter 14 before you make an appointment to visit a loan officer. In today's increasingly impersonal and standardized loan market, it is far more important to choose a competent and considerate loan officer at a reputable institution than to base your choice on a comparison of the **loans** offered by different lenders.

Don't Rush to Refinance

After you have researched the loan market, chosen a loan officer and received an estimate of the closing costs you will be charged, compare the benefits you'll get by refinancing to those of other methods of equity conversion. You may find that there is another way to obtain the cash you need with lower loan fees or terms better suited to your needs.

Advantages of Refinancing

- Receive cash for part of your equity.
- Change to a more attractive, economical or stable loan.

Disadvantages of Refinancing

- The cost to refinance is considerable.
- You must be able to prove that your income is stable and sufficient to repay the loan. In other words, you must be able to qualify for the loan.

5

Equity Loans

An EQUITY LOAN is designed to provide cash for a portion of the owner's equity in a home. It is usually a second mortgage loan, one that is obtained after the primary financing and so is in "second position".

Equity Loans have become very popular in recent years, ever since the 1986 Tax Reform Act reduced (and finally eliminated) the tax deductibility of interest on personal debt, such as car loans and credit card purchases. Since most home mortgage interest is still deductible (with certain noteworthy limits and exceptions outlined in chapter 15), the equity loan offers borrowers a chance to use loans with tax-deductible interest to purchase everything from cars to a Caribbean cruise. No wonder equity loans have suddenly become big business. They've become yet another benefit of home ownership.

Before you fall prey to the lure of the equity loan advertisements in your bank lobby, study the benefits and drawbacks carefully. Equity loans are not necessarily the best route to the riches tied up in your home. Compare these to the other equity conversion methods in this section to determine if this would be the best alternative for you.

Types of Equity Loans

You'll find two main types of equity financing available to you: the Equity Loan and the Equity Line of Credit. With an Equity Loan, the borrower receives the entire amount of the loan at one time; with an Equity Line of Credit, the funds are made available to the borrower, to be withdrawn as needed. In either case, you'll find interest rates to be higher than those on a refinance. You'll also discover that the term of the loan will be considerably shorter: usually 10 or 15 years, rather than 30. This, in turn, makes the monthly payments higher per dollar borrowed on equity loans, since the entire loan must be repaid sooner.

Equity loans were intended to be "second mortgage loans", in other words, designed to be used as an adjunct to an existing home loan ("first mortgage loan"). Because they are usually in "second position"— the second loan recorded against the property— they are somewhat riskier for the lender. Here's why: Should the borrower later default on a loan and a foreclosure sale become necessary, the lender of the first mortgage money (and its lawyers) would be paid first, out of the proceeds of the sale. If any funds remain, the second mortgage lender will be reimbursed. Because of this added risk, the terms and interest rates on equity loans are less generous than those on a refinance. For this reason, if you want to borrow a significant amount of money, a refinance may be more attractive than an equity loan.

Even if you do not have an existing first mortgage loan but wish to borrow a relatively small amount, an equity loan may be right for you. First mortgage lenders often have minimum lending amounts that may be far greater than you need. For a loan of a few thousand dollars, for example, you will probably be directed to the department offering equity loans rather than refinances.

Watch Out for Balloon Payments

Balloon payments are sometimes found on equity loans. This will be outlined in your original loan documents. Instead of making equal monthly payments for the term of the loan, a **balloon payment** clause will require that the loan be paid in full by a certain pre-determined date. Here's how it works: after a few years of regular monthly payments, you'll be expected to pay off the loan in its entirely, with one lump-sum payment. While many equity loans do not carry this provision, be sure to know exactly what your repayment schedule will be before you borrow the funds. Do not consider an equity loan with a balloon payment unless the payoff amount is manageable and you are sure you will have the money on hand to pay it off. Be aware that you risk losing your home if you're not able to come up with the necessary cash. Instead, choose a loan that is fully amortized, with no balloon.

Fixed or Adjustable-Rates Available

Equity loans may have either fixed or adjustable interest rates, depending upon the particular loan and lender. Before making a decision, study the financing information in Chapter 14 of this book and discuss the pros and cons of each type with the loan officer. Interest rate and monthly payments may be lower at first with an adjustable-rate loan but could end up considerably higher before the term is up.

Your Maximum Loan Amount

As in the case of a refinance, the maximum amount you'll be able to borrow will be based upon the value of your home. The requirements will vary from lender to lender and from loan to loan, but usually your total indebtedness (the sum of your first and second mortgage loan, if any, plus your equity loan) may not exceed 70% to 85% of your home's appraised value. That's a vast range, and it gives an indication that it will pay you to comparison shop.

Qualifying For a Second

Lending institutions use the same standards to qualify buyers for equity loans as for first mortgage loans. However, if you have an existing first mortgage loan, your monthly payments for both loans will be added together and the total is used in the calculations. For example, if you already have a loan with monthly payments of $525, and are applying for an equity loan with payments of $175, then the sum of the two, $700, will be used for qualifying. While your loan officer will calculate your borrowing power for you at no charge to you, you'll find qualifying instructions and a worksheet in chapter 14.

What Will it Cost?

Like standard first-mortgage financing, equity loans have closing costs that usually include an appraisal and credit check, a loan fee, mortgagee's title insurance, recording and escrow fees. But because some of these fees are based on the loan amount, the costs for a relatively small equity loan are considerably less than that for a large refinance. As in first mortgage financing, you'll find discount points used to buy down (or buy up) interest rates. (See chapter 14.)

Where to Obtain an Equity Loan

Very often equity loans are available right at the local branch office of your bank. You'll usually find both equity loans and equity lines of credit in the consumer loan departments of lending institutions, rather than in the mortgage lending offices, but this is not true in all cases.

Equity Lines of Credit

If you'd like to have an open account that you can dip into for funds any time they're needed, an equity line of credit may appeal to you. There'll be one loan application and one loan approval, and you'll have access to the equity in your home, to be withdrawn in the amounts you wish, at the times you select. You'll pay interest on only the funds you have borrowed to date. Most equity lines are adjustable-rate loans; that is, they have an interest rate that is evaluated on a regular basis, and changed if the index on which your loan is based has increased or decreased. (You'll find more information about adjustable-rate loans included in Chapter 14.)

There is one significant difference between adjustable-rate equity lines and standard adjustable-rate first mortgage loans: the repayment schedule. With most equity lines, you 'll pay interest only for the first several years (often 10), then amortized payments over a scheduled period of time. You'll pay one loan origination fee or "loan fee" for your equity line of credit, but in addition, you'll pay an often substantial document preparation fee each time you withdraw funds.

Refinances vs Equity Loans

Which would be better for you, a refinance or an equity loan? Sometimes it's a difficult decision.

There's no universal answer, but here are guidelines to help you make an informed choice:

- Consider the interest rate and terms of your first mortgage loan. If the rate is high by today's standards, or if the loan has unattractive features (an adjustable rate, for instance), it may be worth trading in on a whole new (larger) first mortgage loan.

- Consider the amount of cash you need. While you're mulling over the interest rate and terms, take into consideration the size of the "cash-back", especially as it compares to the size of your existing loan. If the cash is a small amount, it may not make sense to choose a major refinance.

- Consider the interest rate, terms, maximum loan amounts and payment amounts on both the refinance and the equity loan. Which will suit your needs better? Get out a calculator and determine your monthly payments (you can use the amortization chart in Appendix II for short-term loans, too), carrying your calculations ahead several years, especially if you're considering an equity loan with a balloon.

- Consider your closing costs. Many of the financing costs associated with either type of loan are based on a percentage of the loan amount. That automatically makes the refinance more expensive than the equity loan since the "refi" would be for a larger amount.

Loan officers can help you determine which method will be most economical and suited to your needs.

Advantage of an Equity Loan

- Equity loans allow homeowners to convert a portion of their equity to cash.

- Borrower can make personal purchases with loans whose interest is tax deductible.

- They allow the buyer to take advantage of a low interest rate on the first mortgage loan, while still providing necessary cash.

Disadvantages of an Equity Loan

- Interest rate is higher than for a first mortgage loan (refinance).

- Term of the loan is shorter.

- Because of these, payments are higher, possibly making it more difficult to qualify for financing.

- Be aware that you cannot convert the full amount of your equity into cash.

6

Reverse Annuity Mortgages

The REVERSE ANNUITY MORTGAGE LOAN allows older homeowners (usually 62 years of age or older) to convert the equity in their home to a cash payment or monthly income from the lender. It differs from an equity loan in that no repayment is required, in most cases, until the home is vacated or sold. Also known as a Reverse Mortgage or Home Equity Conversion Mortgage (HECM).

You may fondly remember the good old days, when you could walk into the neighborhood bank and get a 4% loan on a handshake and your signature. Pretty easy, compared to the hoops you're required to jump through today to get a loan. But financing practices these days aren't all bad. The Reverse Annuity Mortgage is one example of a new trend that's getting better all the time. It is an excellent and eminently practical way to cash in your equity. And after all the years you may have spent "paying off the mortgage" why not let the lender pay **you**, for a change?

In the previous chapters we have looked at two other ways to cash in your equity, through a refinance or an equity loan. But both of these have one serious drawback: the loans must be repaid through regular monthly payments. The prospective borrowers must convince the lender that they have sufficient income to repay the loan and have an impeccable credit history to boot. Those who most need the loan are often unable to qualify.

That's where a reverse mortgage has the edge over a "forward mortgage" such as a refinance or equity loan. Reverse mortgages need not be repaid monthly; they are repaid ultimately through the sale of the home. The owner does not need to demonstrate a gold-plated credit rating or a particular level of income. Equity is the important factor here. If the home is free-and-clear and therefore the owner has ample equity in it, it may be a very good candidate for a reverse mortgage.

There are three types of reverse mortgages available in the U.S.: those insured through the FHA loan program managed by HUD (the federal government's Department of Housing and Urban Development); lender-insured reverse mortgages, which are insured by a private insurance pool; and uninsured reverse mortgages. The FHA-insured loans are by far the most widely spread; they are now offered by lenders in forty-three states and that number has been growing. You are less likely to meet the other two varieties; they are available in very few states. In this chapter we'll take a detailed look at the FHA-insured reverse mortgages— how they work and where to get them— plus an overview of the others types you may encounter.

FHA-Insured Reverse Annuity Mortgages

Thanks to a new program developed during the 1980s by the U.S. Department of Housing and Urban Development (HUD), there's been an increase in awareness about reverse mortgages. This program allows older persons who own homes with little or no existing mortgage debt to receive either monthly payments or a lump-sum cash payment as a loan against the equity their home. No repayment to the lender is necessary as long as the owner continues to live in the home as a principal residence. When the home is sold or the owner vacates it, then the amount of cash that the owner has received, plus interest that has accrued, becomes due and payable. At that time the loan must be repaid in full, usually through the sale of the home, although other funds may be used to pay the loan balance if they are available.

If the value of the home is far greater than the principal and interest amount at the time it is sold, the owner (or the owner's estate) will retain the balance. If, on the other hand, the value of the property has fallen to a level below the total owed in principal and interest, the owner (or the estate) is protected: the lender may not claim more than the value of the property. Any loss to the lender will be covered by FHA insurance. The insurance premiums will added to the loan balance and ultimately paid for by the borrower.

How to Locate a Lender

Although the program is available in the majority of states, some parts of the country have few lenders who offer reverse annuity mortgages. The regional HUD office serving your area can supply the names of lending institutions handling HECMs. If you are need assistance in finding your local HUD office, call HUD headquarters in Washington, D.C.(202-708-1112) and ask for the number of the office nearest you.

How Much Can You Borrow?

The maximum loan amount and the advances received by the borrower are based on a formula that combines several factors: the age of the borrower (or the younger borrower in the case of a couple), the interest rate, and a figure known as the "maximum claim amount." The maximum claim amount is either the appraised value of the home, or what is known as "maximum 203b loan amount for an FHA single-family residence", whichever is less. (The maximum 203b loan amount varies with the location of the property and currently does not exceed $151,725. Your community may have a maximum considerably lower than this. That figure is available from your local HUD office, most real estate agents, and lenders who offer FHA loans, whether or not they offer reverse mortgages or just "forward" FHA loans.).

The age of the borrower also determines the size of advance received. The older the borrower, the larger the payments he or she will receive. The amount of the payments will also depend upon the payment plan chosen by the buyer. There are five different plans, which give the homeowner an option of specifying a particular term, or time period, during which payments will be made. Borrowers can instead request a tenure plan, which will offer them payments as long as they occupy the home as their principal residence. A line of credit plan is available which allows owners to withdraw funds as needed, and there are also combination plans, adding a line of credit to either the term or tenure options.

Since there are a number of choices to be made, often by borrowers who haven't applied for a loan in many years, HUD requires that applicants attend a one-time counseling session that will explain both the HECM program and other alternatives.

Fees and Closing Costs

The fees charged are quite similar to those on a standard loan. They include: an appraisal fee, loan origination fee, mortgage insurance premium, recording and escrow fees, plus a monthly servicing fee. Most or all of these need not be paid in cash; some may be financed with the loan, while others will be added to the loan balance as they are incurred.

Other Types of Reverse Mortgages

While the FHA-insured program is the newest kid on the block and currently the most widely publicized, two other types of reverse mortgage loans are offered in a some areas: Lender-Insured and the Uninsured Reverse Mortgages. There are some important differences between the three programs.

Lender-Insured Reverse Mortgages

Here is a loan that in many ways is similar to the FHA program. It, too, is an insured loan, but with insurance provided by the lender's private "risk pool", financed through premiums paid by borrowers. Like the FHA program, most lender-insured reverse mortgages do not require repayment until the borrower moves out, dies or sells the home. As for the proceeds, there are usually options available for monthly advances or a line of credit, to be used as needed.

One advantage lender-insured reverse mortgages have over the FHA program is their more lenient limits on the size of the loan. FHA's "maximum 203b limit" is conservative and will not allow the owner of a more expensive home to take advantage of all that additional equity. Owners of a $250,000 home, for example, would receive a considerably larger monthly advance with a lender-insured reverse mortgage than with the FHA program.

Uninsured Reverse Mortgages

Unlike the two types of insured reverse mortgages, most uninsured plans are "fixed-term loans"; that is, they have a specific date by which the loan (including the accumulated interest plus loan costs) must be repaid. (If you die, sell or vacate the home before the due date the loan must be repaid immediately.) For many borrowers, that means that they must sell their home in order to repay the loan—whether or not they want to move right at that time. If they fail to pay off the loan when it is due, the lender may foreclose and force the sale of the home.

Think very carefully before choosing an uninsured reverse mortgage. Although you may select a loan term that meets your present needs, will circumstances cause you to change your mind, or your plans? Will you be willing to sell your home by that deadline, no matter what happens in your life? Many borrowers shy away from these loans for that very reason. The risk of losing one's home is significant.

Yet, there are some advantages to the uninsured reverse mortgage loans that make them attractive in a limited number of cases. The size of the monthly advance available is high and loan costs are relatively low, compared to those in insured loan programs. For those borrowers who know, without doubt, that they will be selling their home or will have the funds to repay the loan by the due date, the uninsured reverse mortgage loans can be an acceptable solution to a temporary income shortage.

Advantages of a Reverse Annuity Mortgage

- It's an excellent and affordable way to cash in on equity in a home.

- With insured reverse mortgage programs, the loan need not be repaid until the home is sold or vacated.

- The borrower does not need to qualify for the loan.

- Many more older homeowners can now afford to remain in their homes.

Disadvantages of a Reverse Annuity Mortgage

- In most cases, the home must be sold to pay off the loan (unless other funds are available.)

- The overall financing costs can be high (although borrowers may usually finance most costs, rather than having to pay in cash.)

- Uninsured reverse mortgage programs require the home to be sold as soon as the payment period ends.

- Some programs allow the lender to receive a percentage of the home's appreciation when it is sold.

7

Deferred Payment Loans

If your home is in need of repair or necessary improvements and your income is not sufficiently large to allow to you afford to have the work done, consider a Deferred Payment Loan offered by many local governments or non-profit housing agencies. Here is an example of how one homeowner benefited from this type of financing:

Case History: Repair Now, Pay Later

Marion Johnson suffered a mild stroke recently but is recovering well. Medical expenses played havoc with an already tight budget and Marion did not have the financial resources to pay for minor improvements to her home that would allow her to continue to live there unassisted. She especially needed a grab bar in the shower and a sturdy handrail beside the three steps up to the front porch. To add to her concerns, her home's twenty-one-year-old roof chose this moment to fail, sending a slow drip of water coursing down the fireplace wall whenever it rained.

A friend heard about special no-interest home repair loans offered by the city's community development office. Marion applied for and received a loan of $4800, which covered the cost of a new roof,

*the grab bar and the handrail. To her delight, she
can continue to enjoy her home as long as she
wants to stay. When she does decide to move and
sell her home, the $4800 loan will be repaid out of
the proceeds of the sale. Not a bad deal at all!*

How the Deferred Payment Loan Programs Work

If you meet the eligibility requirements of the program, you may receive a no-interest loan (or very
low interest loan) to pay for essential repairs or
improvements to your home. There are restrictions
to the type of work allowed, but most programs
permit roof and structural work, plumbing and electrical repairs, amenities to meet the needs of a physically disabled person, and weatherization
improvements.

Usually there are no loan fees or closing costs required and, as in any home mortgage financing, a
lien in the amount of the loan will be recorded
against the property. It is not necessary to repay the
loan until you decide to sell or move from your
home. At that time, the loan will be repaid from the
proceeds of the sale of your home. You cannot be
forced to move out early in order to repay the loan,
nor can you "lose your home" as a result of this
financing. Your own equity— the money that you
have invested in your home— will repay the loan
when you sell.

Some deferred loan programs (but certainly not all)
offer a special loan that seems to disappear at just
the right moment! For those borrowers who continue to live in their home a specified number of
years after receiving the loan, the repayment
amount is reduced. According to the terms of some
deferred loans, if you stay there long enough, the
entire amount of the loan may be forgiven and no
repayment is required. Remember that not all de-

ferred payment loan programs are alike, so be sure that you understand exactly what and when you will be required to pay.

Eligibility for Deferred Payment Loans

Eligibility standards vary considerably, from one lender to another. However deferred payment loans are almost always need-based; there is usually a maximum income level that borrowers may not exceed at the time they receive the loan. In addition, you may find a minimum age requirement, although this is not true of many programs. The loans are available to homeowners who have enough equity in their home to qualify; if you have a large first mortgage loan, equity loans or lines of credit, you may find that you are not eligible for your community's deferred loan program.

Where to Apply for a Loan

Unless you're lucky enough to hear about a deferred payment loan program in your area, it may take a bit of effort to track one down. Try calling your city or county government and ask for a housing commission or development department. Most state governments have agencies that deal with housing issues, often called the "Housing" or "Community Development" division. These may be able to direct you to local agencies offering deferred loan programs. They are certainly well worth the hunt!

Advantages of a Deferred Payment Loan

• No interest (or a minimal interest rate) charged.

• Usually no loan fees or closing costs charged.

• No payment required until you move or sell your home.

- Some programs offer to forgive a portion (or all) of the loan if you continue to live in the home for a specified number of years.

Disadvantages of a Deferred Payment Loan

- Not available in all communities.

- Sometimes difficult to find a source for these loans.

- The loan must be paid when you move, die or sell your home. If you plan to bequeath your home to an heir who wants to live in the home, the loan must still be repaid at your death. (It may be paid off without selling the home if other funds are available.)

- If you receive a deferred payment loan (or any other home loan), your may not qualify for a reverse annuity mortgage.

8

Other Ways to
Cash in Your Equity

So far, in this book, we've taken a detailed look at several ways to turn your equity into ready cash, through refinancing your home, by obtaining an equity loan, reverse annuity mortgage, or a deferred payment loan. But there are still other techniques that can be used to help extract the money your home owes you. For instance, chapters 9, 10 and 11 will cover the fine art of selling your home, one way to cash in on **all** of your equity. Then, in Part V, the Tax Considerations section, two different methods of equity conversion appear: chapter 17 offers an indirect approach, through a charitable gift of your home coupled with the benefit of a life estate. Chapter 18 will describe the advantages of property tax deferral, for those homeowners fortunate enough to live in areas of the country where this program is available.

That leaves another method of equity conversion: a **sale with a leaseback**. At first glance, it seems as though this surely belongs in the chapter devoted to selling your home, and indeed it is a true sale. Yet this method also offers homeowners a way to continue to enjoy life in their present home, and that's what this section of the book is all about.

How to Sell and Stay Put

Simply put, a sale with a leaseback works this way: you sell your home to an investor who allows you to lease the property throughout your lifetime. You, the seller, finance the sale; you receive a down payment and regular monthly purchase payments from the buyer. You, in turn, pay the new owner rent each month.

Let me say immediately that this method is not widely used. It can be cumbersome, rather unappealing and very difficult for most homeowners to put into practice. But it deserves to be mentioned because with some properties, it works very well. In one case, an elderly homeowner lived in an old farmhouse on ten acres of land, right in the path of future development. He was able to negotiate the sale of his land (with a leaseback) to a developer who had created an elaborate new housing tract on one side, and who was anxious to tie up the surrounding property. The investor was willing to wait because the property was valuable to him and would greatly increase in value in the next few years.

Most homes simply do not have magnetic appeal to investors. The tax benefits that can be realized by such a transaction are not attractive enough to make every home desirable. However, if you own a home that has outstanding future potential because of its size, location, acreage, proximity to development, or unique characteristics, this type of sale may be excellent for you. To put it to work, you will need an attorney who specializes in real estate matters, a real estate agent who works closely with either commercial or residential developers (depending upon the probable use of your property) and an accountant who is well acquainted with this technique.

Part III
SELL YOUR HOME
SUCCESSFULLY

Part III
SELL YOUR HOME
SUCCESSFULLY

Each week, throughout the United States, close to 800,000 people move. Is it your turn this year? If you're a homeowner who's eager to pick up and start a new life in a new home, this section of the book is being written with you in mind, for the first hurdle you'll cross is the sale of your home.

While it is always "cleaner" and smoother to sell your home first and then look for another, with cash in your pocket ready to buy, it is not always practical to do so. Or smart, for that matter. If you feel rushed into buying because you must give the new owner possession of your old home, you won't be making level-headed decisions. So it's a far better plan to research your housing options while you are preparing to sell your home. If you are intending to both sell and buy, or if you're simply contemplating both a sale and a purchase, sit down and read Parts III and IV, to discover how to do both with great success.

9

Should You Sell Your Home?

Selling your home is the ultimate way to cash in on the equity you've built up over the years. And it's the only way to receive cash for close to the entire amount of your equity. At the same time, it is a decision that is difficult to reverse. Unlike an equity loan or a refinance, selling a home calls for heavy-duty decision making.

Should you sell your present home? This is often a tough question to answer because emotions interfere with reasoning power. The results seem so overwhelmingly final. If you're having a difficult time making that decision, allow yourself to re-phrase the question in this way: "Should I sell my home **now**?" By adding the word "now", you've reduced the scope of your decision and given yourself some breathing room to plan for your future.

Because selling your home is a serious emotional and financial consideration, spend plenty of time making the right decision, one based on facts and research. Here are some points to consider carefully **before** you come to a conclusion:

1. *What is a reasonable asking price for your home?*

It is not easy for most of us to judge our own home's market value impartially. You may feel that your house is a cut above (or below) similar homes in your neighborhood, but the amenities that appeal to you may not be particularly important to the average buyer. So it's wise to obtain an impartial estimate of value from a professional real estate agent or appraiser.

Real estate agents are usually happy to provide a **comparative market analyis** at no charge to you, if they understand that you will consider listing your home with them whenever you are ready to sell. However, you are under no obligation to list. Emphasize that you are, at the moment, determining whether or not to sell and are not ready to list your home immediately. It is reasonable (and smart) to ask three different agents for an estimate of value, so that you can compare not only the value, but also the techniques used in determining it.

A **fee appraisal** from a licensed appraiser is not usually necessary, but if the reports from the three agents varied widely in price or if you simply did not feel comfortable with the value or techniques used, a fee appraisal may be money well spent. It is sometimes very difficult to determine the fair market value of a home, especially if the design is unusual or if the home differs from all others in the neighborhood. If you choose to pay for a fee appraisal, the cost will be around $350 to $400, with an additional charge for large homes or those involving travel time. A loan officer, real estate agent, or real estate attorney can suggest names of qualified appraisers who work with residential property.

2. *Consider Your Local Market Conditions.*

Real estate agents can supply information about the real estate market in your neighborhood. You'll want to know how quickly homes like yours are selling, how many comparable homes have sold recently, and at what final sales price. Find out also how many homes are on the market now in your neighborhood, how long they've been listed and at what listing price. Ask agents how available financing is for buyers and what your chances of receiving cash will be.

An interesting statistic to look at— and one that can be supplied by most real estate agents— is the comparison of recent sales prices to the final asking price in your area. It is usually expressed as a percentage. If you discover, for example, that homes are selling, on average, at 95% of their final asking price and taking four months to do so, you can evaluate the strength of the market. You won't be expecting an instant sale at full price, but will allow sufficient time and negotiating room in your asking price.

3. *Determine Payoff Figures For Your Loans*

If you have a mortgage loan, an equity loan or any other loans secured by your home, write to your lenders to let them know that you are considering selling your home and to ask for payoff information on your loans. Be sure to include your loan account numbers and your signature, as borrower. This letter serves three purposes. First, the loan payoff information you receive will allow you to estimate what your proceeds would be if you decide to sell. Second, by asking your lender in the letter whether the loan is assumable or if the home may be sold on contract (and what fees and requirements the lender has for such a sale), you'll know in advance of an offer what your options are in this respect.

Finally, by notifying your lender of your intention to sell, you may be satisfying a requirement found on a few older loans. These particular loans carry a substantial interest penalty if the lender is not notified in advance of a payoff. While your chances today of still having such a loan are slim, be on the safe side and notify your lender when you put your home on the market.

4. What will your closing or settlement costs be?

While the buyer usually bears the brunt of the costs in most transactions when a new loan is involved, sellers do not escape unscathed. If you haven't sold a home recently, you may be quite surprised to find that the settlement costs are higher than you expected. A real estate agent can give you an estimate of your closing costs, which will include some or all of the following: escrow and recording fees, property tax prorates, owner's title insurance premium, sales tax, transfer tax, reconveyance fee and real estate commission. (For a detailed list of both sellers' and buyers' closing costs, see the worksheet in chapter 14.)

In addition to these standard fees, you may be asked to pay for repairs to your home, especially if the buyer is obtaining a new loan from an outside source. Lenders can be picky; the appraisal and the buyer's home inspection can reveal an amazing array of defects in a home that is basically sound. You can help limit the impact of unexpected costs by stating in writing when youreceive an offer to purchase, that you are willing to pay up to a certain figure (we'll use $500 as an example) for repairs if required by the lender. If the buyer agrees to this figure and later the lender's demands carry a $700 price tag, the buyer will be required to pay the $200 difference in order for the sale to be consummated.

So when you're calculating your closing costs, be sure to build in a cushion for repairs.

5. *What will your tax liability be, if you sell your home?*

Before you reach a decision about selling your home, be sure you know the tax consequences of a sale. A good general knowledge is not enough. So often sellers think they know the tax laws pertaining to capital gains, only to discover on April 15th that they've missed out on significant tax savings by selling a day too early or a week too late. Start by reading Part VI of this book, TAX CONSIDERATIONS, then discuss your specific plans with your accountant before you make a move.

6. *How much cash can you reasonably expect to receive from the sale of your home, after all closing costs and taxes are paid?*

There's no quick answer to this question, so don't be tempted to throw out a figure and assume it's close. Once you've worked your way through all of the preceding questions, if you've accurately researched the market value of your home, market conditions and trends, payoff figures on loans secured by the home, plus determined a close estimate of your closing costs and tax liability, you can complete the worksheet by calculating the bottom line: the amount of cash you'll be able to pocket after the sale.

Other Factors to Consider

The decision to sell your home is not based on the financial proceeds alone. Other factors have to be taken into consideration. Emotions play a big part in real estate decisions of this type, and understandably so. You may be torn, for example, between a wish to live a carefree retirement in a sunny resort community and sadness at leaving family, old friends and plenty of memories behind. While emotions often provide the most compelling reasons to sell, be sure that you are supporting your emotional whims with good, solid research. Double-check your calculations and give your decision plenty of time to gel before you rush to sell.

What Will Your New Housing Cost?

Another point to consider before putting your home on the market is the cost of your new housing. Whether you are planning to buy another home after yours sells, or rent an apartment, be sure that you know to the penny the costs involved. It is not enough to tell yourself, for instance, "I know I'll be able to get a nice apartment for around $500 a month." Or, "I should be able to find a 2-bedroom condo for $75,000."

Before you put your home on the market, you should know exactly what that $500, or $75,000, will cover. Have you looked at actual homes for rent or sale in the neighborhood where you'd like to live? Are those prices likely to change by the time your home is sold? Will availability (or, rather, lack of it) push prices higher? What other costs will be involved? (Association fees, closing costs, storage fees, moving expenses?) Don't be caught by surprise, after you've agreed to sell your home.

Should You Rent Your Home Instead of Selling?

If you find that you are reluctant to sell your home because of strong emotional ties or other reasons, consider the pros and cons of holding on to your existing home but renting it for awhile, until you're ready to cut the ties permanently.

Home Seller's Worksheet

Use this handy worksheet to estimate the net proceeds from the sale of your home:

A. Probable asking price of home: $_____

B. Estimated sales price: $_____
    (allow room for negotiation)

_____

C. Estimated selling time:_____
    (include 4 to 10 weeks after you accept
    an offer for buyer's loan processing.)

_____

D. Payoff figures for existing loans: Loan I: $_____

                                          Loan II:_____

                                          Loan III:_____

                                          Total: $_____

E. Estimated closing costs: _____
    (include real estate commission)

F. Estimated cost of repairs: _____

G. Tax on capital gains: $_____

H. Add D + E + F + G: $_____

_____

Your net proceeds from the sale of your home: _____
    (line B minus line H)

_____

Advantages to Renting Your Home vs Selling

- Once you sell out of a market, it is expensive to buy again if you should change your mind.

- This plan gives you flexibility if you think you may want to return.

- You'll receive a monthly income from the rent payments.

- Your home is appreciating in value (with luck and a solid real estate market), so that it may be worth more when you eventually sell it.

- If the real estate market is slow, you'll be able to sit it out and wait for a better time to sell.

Disadvantages to Renting Your Home

- You'll still be required to pay taxes and upkeep.

- Long-distance landlording is not easy. Repairs, maintenance, rent-collection and general management are difficult to oversee from another state or town.

- If you hire a property-management company to rent and maintain the home, your monthly income is reduced.

- If you plan to use your $125,000 capital gains exclusion (see Chapter 17 for details), you'll have to be very careful that you meet the residency requirements to the day. You may find that you'll have to move back temporarily to satisfy the tax laws, or forfeit your exclusion.

- Your equity in the home will be more difficult to convert to cash if you are renting it rather than using it as your principal residence. Interest rates and ratios on refinances and equity loans for rental property are not nearly as attractive as those for your own home and lenders today are reluctant to offer "cash out" financing on rental property (where the owner pockets the cash instead of using the loan to pay off an existing loan).

• It is unlikely that you will be able to use the rental house as security for a Reverse Annuity Mortgage.

• You are likely to forfeit such benefits as property tax deferral (see Chapter 18) or special repair loans for owner-occupied property.

The Decision to Sell

If you've done your research well, totalled up the pros and taken the cons into consideration, you have reached a decision based on a realistic assessment of your needs and market conditions. The following chapter covers the information you'll need to know to sell successfully and get your new life off to a splendid start.

10

Working with a Real Estate Agent

Older homeowners, especially those with some real estate experience under their belt and time on their hands, are often tempted to sell their home by themselves, without the help of a real estate agent. Some are successful; many are not as successful as they would like to be. Should you work with an agent or "go it alone"? That decision is yours to make, of course, but this chapter will give you the pros and cons of working with an agent, plus valuable tips on how to develop a successful business relationship with your agent that gets your home sold quickly and profitably.

If you haven't sold a home in recent years— or if you've never sold one— you'll learn about the changes taking place today in real estate practices. New trends in seller- and buyer-representation will be covered in detail and in the following chapter, you'll hear about new questions of liability that affect both sellers and buyers.

Should You Work With an Agent?

Should you work with an agent? I'll tell you what I would do if I were selling my own home today. For years, I actively sold real estate and I still maintain my license, although I no longer work directly with buyers and sellers. Would I advertise and sell my own home? No, because a good agent can do two things better than I can: first, agents who are actively working in my neighborhood can give my home far better exposure than I can. I simply could not easily attract the number of qualified buyers an agent can. Secondly, I am too emotionally attached to my home to be dispassionate in my negotiations with a buyer. After all, this is **my** home, **my** equity and **my** profit we're discussing; I find that I have far greater strength as a seller if I instruct my agent and stay out of the fray myself.

If you have a ready and willing buyer standing in the wings, waiting to buy your home for whatever price you set, that's a different matter. Since no marketing or negotiations are necessary, you may prefer to ask an attorney (preferably one adept at real estate matters), rather than a real estate agent, to prepare the documents and protect your interests in the transaction.

Selling Your Home by Yourself

Are you tempted to try selling your home by yourself? Being a FSBO can sometimes work out well. FSBO (pronounced FIZZ-BOH) stands for **For Sale By Owner** in real estate jargon. FSBOs are homeowners who sell their homes themselves, without the help of an agent.

Sometimes, FSBOs can be quite successful, especially in an area that's experiencing a real estate boom. But there are problems that are frequently encountered by FSBOs. One is, as I've mentioned, the difficulty in advertising and attracting the attention of a sufficient number of buyers (after all, a FSBO has only one property to show.) It's hard, time-consuming work to write ads, prepare sales literature, show a home, negotiate offers, arrange financing and handle the necessary documentation. If you have a hankering to be a FSBO, be sure to retain an attorney to help you avoid the many pitfalls that can occur in your real estate transaction.

The one big advantage of the do-it-yourself approach is that FSBOs save the substantial cost of the real estate commission (often 6% or 7% of the sales price). But it's not all gravy: FSBOs usually must spend considerable money and effort in trying to achieve their goal. Advertising is particularly expensive for a FSBO. Real estate firms negotiate discounts with newspapers since they are frequent, high-volume advertisers. They buy blocks of space or even full pages at bargain prices, while FSBOs pay top dollar for a one-inch ad in the classifieds. Then too, FSBOs must pay the cost of their ads, whether or not they are ultimately successful in finding a buyer. Compare this to sellers who list with a real estate agent: in most cases, their ads are the agent's expense, with no cost to the seller unless the home is sold. So unless the market is booming, you may find the commission less expensive in the long run.

One good thing about becoming a FSBO: you don't have to look hard to find a real estate agent, should you change your mind and want to work with one. If you market your home yourself, you'll soon get to know most of the agents in your neighborhood. As soon as you hammer the sign in the front yard and your first ad appears in the Sunday paper, agents will call and stop by to offer their services. It's a good opportunity for you to meet the agents and— who knows? There may come a time when you're ready to work with one.

How to Choose the Right Agent for You

If you have not previously worked with a real estate agent who you'd like to work with again, start by asking friends and neighbors for the names of real estate companies or agents that they might recommend. Make a list of agents who are active in your neighborhood, those whose names appear frequently on For Sale signs on homes nearby. Study the real estate section of your local newspaper to see how companies with homes listed in your neighborhood present themselves. If you're pleased with the image or tone of a certain company, add its name to your list.

Now that you've compiled your list of possible real estate agents or companies, the second step is to interview likely candidates. Meet these people in their offices, or— even better— invite them, individually, to visit your home. You'll find that by talking to real estate agents, you'll see a difference in style. Personalities differ. An agent who is highly recommended by a friend may not be the best choice for you. Find a competent person you enjoy working with.

Not All Agents are REALTORS®

As you interview, you'll also be looking for certain characteristics. Professionalism is important, but also look for enthusiasm and a willingness to work hard. Talk to these real estate agents about their background and experience selling homes like yours. Don't hesitate to ask for references. Find out about the company they work for. Are the firm and the agent members of the local Board of REALTORS®? Only real estate agents who belong to the National and State Association of REALTORS®, and the local Board of REALTORS® are permitted to call themselves REALTORS®. So not every real estate agent is a REALTOR®. Those who are must agree to conform to a strict code of ethics in all their real estate dealings.

Evaluating the Real Estate Firm

When you're interviewing agents, ask if they belong to a **Multiple Listing Service**, if there is one in your community. Membership in a Multiple Listing Service makes it easier for agents to show properties listed by other member firms. Multiple Listing Services publish books and a computer database on all the homes listed by members. The cost for this service is carried by the real estate firm, not the seller, and is excellent exposure for your home. It can greatly increase your home's availability to potential buyers.

As you interview the real estate agents, learn how they work with sellers, what services they provide and what you can expect them to do when your home is on the market. Sellers often ask the question, "Which is better, a large real estate firm or a small one?" As long as the firm is able and willing to provide adequate service, then the size of the company is immaterial. You'll want to be certain that the firm will advertise your home adequately and give it excellent exposure. Find a reputable firm, ask detailed questions about the service you'll be getting, and concentrate on choosing a professional from that company who will be competent and congenial to work with.

The Wrong Reason to Choose an Agent

You have good reason to be sceptical of an agent who promises you a unusually high sales price and a quick sale. No agent can promise that. While it may be tempting to choose the agent who offers to list (and sell) your home at top dollar, be sure that the agent's estimates of value are backed up by solid market research. Study the documentation and decide for yourself if your home can be expected to command that high a price.

It's far better policy to choose an agent based on his or her marketing plan. In short, what will your agent do for you and your home in order to achieve your goal of a quick, profitable sale?

What Agents Should Do for Sellers

- Become very familiar with your home and its amenities.

- Prepare a detailed comparative market analyis (CMA) to show you how your home compares to others in your neighborhood that have sold recently and those currently on the market.

- Help you determine the best possible asking price.

- Outline clearly and specifically a marketing plan for your home.

- Give you advice on how to prepare your home for showings.

- Draw up and explain the listing agreement in detail.

- Prepare a flier or other sales literature.

- Advertise your home as agreed to.

- Show your home to prospective buyers and make follow-up calls to them as needed.

- Report back to you regularly.

- Market your home according to the terms of your listing agreement and the details of your marketing plan.

- Prepare and negotiate offers or counter-offers according to your instructions.
- Help buyers obtain financing.
- Assist the fee appraiser in determining the fair market value.
- Keep the paperwork moving towards escrow.
- Coordinate the closing or settlement— and attend it with you.
- Help you turn over possession to the buyers.

Whom Do Agents Really Represent?

Until recently, most of the agents specializing in residential real estate were seller's agents. That is, they were employed by the sellers to represent them in the sale of the home. It is easy to think of your listing agent in this capacity, but another agent who shows your home to a prospective buyer may also legally be representing you, the seller, not the buyer. This is true even if you have never met the agent, and even if the agent and the buyer are close friends. The majority of residential real estate agents today are seller's agents, but recently there has been a dramatic increase in the number of buyer's agents, agents who represent the interests of the buyer, rather than the seller. Another new trend in the residential marketplace is the idea of dual agency, where one brokerage firm represents both the seller and the buyer in the transaction.

Does it really make a difference to you, as a seller, who the agent legally represents? In actual practice, it may not. While agents have a fiduciary relationship with the party they represent, they also have a responsibility to be fair and honest to the other party in the transaction. But if a buyer's agent shows your property to a client, be aware that anything you say to that agent must legally be related to the buyer. If the agent represents the buyers, be cautious about what you say in their agent's presence. Avoid playing into the buyers' hands by making statements like, "I've got to sell this home quickly and I'd probably come down off my asking price by about $10,000 if I have to."

How Agents Are Paid

Agents normally work on a commission basis. That is, they do not receive a weekly pay check, but instead are paid a percentage of the sales price of the home when it is sold. Traditionally, the seller pays the commission, which is then divided into two portions: known as the Listing Commission and the Selling Commission. Often two real estate firms are involved in a transaction. An agent from Company ABC may have listed your home, while an agent from another firm, XYZ Realty, may have shown the property to buyers and written their offer. In this case, Company ABC would receive the Listing Commission, while XYZ Realty receives the Selling Commission. The two agents involved are each paid a certain percentage of their company's portion.

If the buyers are represented by a buyer's agent, the selling commission is usually deducted from the sales price of the home, and the seller will pay only the listing commission to his or her agent. (Some buyer's agents however accept payment in the traditional way, through a commission split.) Either way, the cost to you is the same.

Agents are paid only when a sale is completed. Since selling a home requires a considerable investment of your agent's time, energy and money, be sure that you give your agent all possible assistance in putting together a transaction. Allow the agent a reasonable time limit on the listing agreement; if the average sale in your neighborhood takes 102 days, give your agent **at least** that length of listing. That's only fair, and if you've chosen your agent carefully, a three- to six-month listing will not be a problem.

Most of the difficulties that crop up between sellers and their real estate agents come from a difference of expectations. It's very important that you and your agent discuss exactly what roles each of you will play in the sale of your home. Before you sign a listing agreement, know what to expect from your agent in the way of advertising, home showings, open houses, and ongoing contact with you. Communication is essential to a good working relationship.

Once you've chosen an agent, you're ready to get down to the business of putting your home on the market. The next chapter will focus on the selling process— how to make it quick, painless and profitable.

11

Sell Successfully and Profitably

Once you've decided to sell your home, there's no point in pussyfooting around. Put it on the market and get it sold as quickly, effortlessly and profitably as possible. This chapter will show you how to do just that.

Factors that Spell Success or Failure

There are three important factors that determine the saleability of your home: **location, condition** and **price.** In times of high interest rates and a slow real estate market, I would add a fourth factor: **terms,** by which I mean the availability of special financing and other considerations that make your home particularly easy to buy. If you want your home to sell quickly, at the highest possible price, you must pay close attention to all of these elements when you get ready to put your home on the market.

We'll take a look at how each of these influences your home's saleability and what you can do to slant the odds in your favor. No home is inherently **un-**saleable; only when the determining factors are out of balance will a home sit without a buyer.

Play up the Location for All It's Worth

Of the three primary factors that control selling success, only one— location— is beyond your control. You and your prospective buyers will just have to accept the location as is. But if your home's location seems less than desirable, don't assume you'll never be able to sell it. Think positive! Remember, what one buyer considers appalling, another may find appealing. For example, if your home is right at a busy intersection, you'll want to find a buyer who will appreciate living "Right on the bus line" or "Close to shopping". While this location would be a drawback for some, accessibility is an attractive feature for many buyers. Still others will find a busy intersection acceptable if the home is priced right and is in excellent condition.

A difficult location simply requires creative marketing tactics and an emphasis on those other sales factors that **are** well within your control: condition, price and terms.

Condition Your Home to Sell

The physical appearance of your home sends a message to a prospective buyer, from the outside landscaping and paint colors, to the inside decor and warmth. What message will your home send? It may not be the message you hope to convey. It's very difficult to be objective about one's own home. After years of living in it, we're apt to overlook all sorts of less-than-perfect sights, from the peeling trim on the window frames to the clutter of the knicknack shelf.

Before you put your home on the market, stand back and really look at it with a critical eye, from an outsider's point of view. Start outside. Go across the street and take a good look. What would you see if you were a buyer? Real estate agents use the term **curb appeal** to refer to the first impression that a home creates. Does your home have lots of curb appeal? Will the prospective buyer see a freshly painted front door, neatly trimmed lawn and sparkling windows? Or is your flower bed blooming with weeds? That first impression is critical. If your home lacks curb appeal, not even the best real estate agent can coax buyers to see inside.

Now ring the doorbell and walk through your front doorway, as though you were visiting the home for the first time. (Did the doorbell work and did the door swing open smoothly without hitting furniture?) Look at the views from each window, consider the condition of carpet and walls. Open the closet doors. Turn on the faucets, look over the ceilings for signs of leaks, evaluate the cupboards in the kitchen. In fact, do everything a conscientious buyer would do.

Very, very few of us live in a way that makes our home perfect for showing. Even if your home is spotlessly clean and decorated beautifully, it may not be sending the right message to prospective buyers. Here are a few tricks the experts use to help a buyer feel right at home.

Guerilla Tactics for Showings

- First, pack away, stash away or give away at least one-third of your furniture and two thirds of your accessories. Your rooms will grow instantly larger— at least to the buyer's eye— and your home's value will increase accordingly. A home that is heavily decorated with family memorabilia will convey the subtle message that this is **your** home; would-be buyers will have a difficult time imagining themselves living there.

- Make sure that the entire house looks absolutely clean. Carpets should be freshly sham-
pooed, walls washed or painted and floors
scrubbed. Windows must sparkle; your home
will look larger when buyers can see the yard
easily. If you were to spend any money or effort in getting a home ready to show, this is
where to spend it first. The return on your investment will be well worth it!

- Watch out for odors! If you have pets or a
smoker in residence, be especially conscious of
this. Smells are your personal stamp; buyers
can't feel "at home" in a house that smells as
though it belongs to someone else. It never
hurts to bake bread (frozen dough makes it
easy) or gingerbread just before a showing. Or
simmer a stick of cinnamon and a few cloves in
a pot of water. Aromas like these say "Home"—
and that's exactly the message you want to convey to the buyer.

- Open all the drapes and turn on the lights. One
seller taught me an interesting tactic: he used
pink lightbulbs in his living room and bedroom
lamps. They cast a very flattering light on the
room and its occupants.

- Light a fire in the fireplace, unless the weather
is hot.

- Remove half of your dishes from the shelves of
your kitchen cupboards and pack them away.
Do the same with your pots and pans, spices
and canned goods. Each drawer in your
kitchen should be no more than one-third to
one-half full of flatware or linens. (Where do
you put the extras? The attic is fine; even a garage is acceptable. Prospective buyers have no

trouble overlooking a garage with packing boxes in it.)

- Work the same magic on your bathrooms. It's amazing to hear buyers say, "There's lots of cupboard space in this house!"— when you know very well there isn't nearly enough!
- Listen to what your home is saying. Do the stairs creak? Does the screen door stick? Will the furnace fan whine every now and then? Fix them before you put your home on the market. One negative noise will say to a buyer, "This house hasn't been perfectly maintained. Don't you wonder what else may be wrong with it?"

Hide Your Valuables

When you put your home on the market, hide or remove anything valuable or dangerous: jewelry or coin collections, firearms and prescription drugs. Breakable objects should be put away. They can be fascinating to a buyer's children, but a source of worry to the parents. If the buyers are feeling concerned about maneuvering their offspring through the perils of the living room, it will keep them from concentrating on the positive features and will leave them with an uneasy feeling about your home. Remove temptation wherever possible.

Where to Spend Your Money

Be cautious about spending money just to get your home sold. Extensive remodeling shortly before a sale rarely gives a 100% return on money invested. Many remodeling projects actually yield a surprisingly small return, or none at all. You will be far wiser to spend money on a general clean-up and a few specific "hot spots" that will catch a buyer's attention. A home that looks well cared for will be very reassuring to prospective buyers.

Sellers frequently wonder how much time, effort and money to pour into a home just before a sale. Here are the questions most commonly asked:

Should I hire professionall landscaper?

Curb appeal is worth spending some money on. But an elaborate landscape job is usually unnecessary, and is rarely cost-effective. Your home should have a front yard and entry that is well groomed, and maintained to a level that is at least equal to the other homes in the neighborhood. Add pizzazz with a large pot of annuals beside the front door, or a colorful bed of flowers beside the walk.

Is it a good idea to paint the exterior?

If the color is dated or unattractive, certainly paint the siding. Otherwise, paint the entire house only if it is peeling, or is badly weathered. Try painting just the trim and front door first; that may be all it takes to spiff up the exterior.

Must I replace the carpet?

Again, if it is clearly an outdated style, a loud color, or badly worn or stained, replace it with a neutral, non-patterned carpet. Otherwise, a thorough cleaning will suffice.

Should I paint the interior?

Neutral is the operative word here. If your walls are a neutral, light color and in good condition, don't bother to paint. But it is money well spent to lighten up dark rooms or replace old wallpaper with a neutral coat of paint.

What about new wallpaper?

Not a good idea unless you have stubborn old wallpaper that refuses to peel off. Patterned wallcoverings are so very **definite**: what appeals to you may not be attractive to a prospective buyer. You are much better off painting walls off-white and saving your money.

Should I replace the roof?

This brings up the question of whether you are **maintaining** value or **increasing** value. Buyers expect to buy a home with a roof that doesn't leak; that's a basic presumption. So repair a leaking roof and replace it if it cannot be repaired. But if you spend an extra $4,000 to install a deluxe new roof instead of a standard quality roof, will you be increasing the value of your home by $4,000? Probably not. You may not be increasing the value of your home at all, but instead you're simply maintaining the value that all buyers expect.

What about adding a second bathroom?

The best advice is this: don't rush into any major expense, until you have thoroughly researched your market. You are usually better off adjusting the price to compensate for the lack of the second bathroom than spending the money to add one just for the new owners. Let **them** do the work!

Here's where real estate agents can be of help. They can give you an objective viewpoint. They know what attracts prospective buyers and what the current standards are for homes in your neighborhood. They can help you determine if you're likely to recover the cost of any renovation you're considering. Many additions increase the **asking price** of a home without actually increasing the **value** to a potential buyer.

If the Price is Right, It Will Sell

The third factor that will determine your home's saleability is your asking price. Set the price too high and your home will sit on the market for months or even years. Set your price too low and you cheat yourself of well-earned profits.

It is very hard for sellers to be objective. Most of us have strong emotional ties to our home. Most sellers base their asking price on what they feel they need or want to get from their home, rather than what a buyer is willing to pay for it. But to sell your home quickly and profitably you must base your judgment on facts, rather than emotion. The only way to determine a fair market value for your home is to research the real estate activity in your neighborhood.

If you have followed the research suggestions outlined in Chapter 9, you know which other homes in your neighborhood have sold recently or are for sale now, and what their selling and asking prices have been. You are now in a position to be able to reach an educated judgment about the market value of your home.

"I Can Afford to Wait..."

If you are under no time constraints, it may be tempting to you to set a sky-high asking price, then sit back and wait for an offer. This is a poor strategy for several reasons.

First, research shows that under reasonable market conditions, your home has its greatest chance of being sold during the first thirty days it is on the market. New properties attract by far the most attention. Secondly, when buyers and agents take a close look at your home and discover that your sales price is far too high, your home will be classified unofficially as an "overpriced turkey". Prospective buyers will compare your property with other similar homes and will quickly decide that yours is not a good value. Your home will sit on the market and grow stale, at least in the eyes of buyers. It will still be shown, but usually as an example of how well priced the listing down the street is, compared to yours!

When it eventually does sell, your price may be considerably less than what you might have received had you priced it correctly. Statistics show that the longer a home sits on the market, the lower the final sales price will be, compared to its asking price. There is a "right price" for your home; it is to your advantage to determine what that price is before the For Sale sign goes up in the yard.

Leave Room to Negotiate

When you set the price of your home, be sure to leave a little bit of room to negotiate. It's human nature to be happier if you've struck a bargain, and buyers are no exception to that rule. If you hold out for the full price, the buyers will often react later in the transaction by being difficult to deal with on other matters. So build some goodwill into your asking price; allow a little room to "deal". Whether you build in a cushion of $1000, $5000 or $10,000 will depend upon the pace of the market, the price of your home and the negotiating customs in your community. An experienced real estate agent can be of help when you're determining where to set the price.

When to Allow Showings

The more readily accessible your home is for a showing, the greater its chances of selling. That doesn't mean you have to give up your private life to have your home available 24 hours a day. For instance, if you're having a dinner party, allow yourself to say 'No' to a request for a showing at that time. But don't make unnecessary restrictions about showing times. Out-of-town buyers or those who must make a quick decision may not be around tomorrow.

Maximum exposure does produce better results. That applies to the presence of a For Sale sign in the front yard and a secure lockbox to hold the housekey. Your agent will supply this lockbox, which makes more showings possible. Once you make the commitment to sell your home, give it all you've got.

Should You Be Present for Showings?

When a real estate agent makes an appointment for a showing, turn on lights and soft background music, then leave before the prospective buyers and the agent arrive. The reason for this is purely psychological: if prospective buyers walk into your home and meet you, the owner, they will identify that home with you. It's **your** home. How much better it would be to have them start thinking of it as **their** home, not yours! That's what happens if you're not around. With just their agent present, the buyers will be less inhibited and will feel more like spending time "trying on the home for size".

Showing Advice for FSBOs

If you are a FSBO and not working with a real estate agent, you'll have to be present at showings, of course. Try to be as unobtrusive as possible. Give the buyers plenty of elbow room and time to wander in the yard without you hovering nearby.

Prepare an information sheet about your home that prospective buyers can take with them. It should include a photograph and a list of all the facts and figures they'll want to consider. The flier will help them remember your home as they look at dozens of other properties.

Security Precautions for Showings

Theft and physical attack during showings are problems too prevalent to be dismissed as insignificant. Earlier in this chapter, I stressed the importance of hiding smaller valuables and drugs. This advice is worth repeating. If your home is filled with large items of value, you may want to consider not permitting your agent to hold Open Houses, where anyone may walk in from the street to plan a future break-in.

Unless you're a FSBO, make it a rule **never** to show your home without an agent present to would-be buyers who ring your doorbell asking to see it. Smile, hand them a flier, offer to make an appointment with the agent, but don't invite them in. Let your agent qualify them and take any risk. After all, security is one excellent reason for working with an agent.

Qualifying a Prospective Buyer

It's been estimated that, on the average, people look at 20 to 30 homes before they decide to put an offer on one and when they're narrowing down choices, most buyers will want to look again at a home two or three times before making their final decision. You may have several potential buyers looking at your home each week. As you tidy up for yet another showing, you may wonder if all of those visitors can possibly afford your home. Are they really qualified buyers or are they just plain curious?

Most competent real estate agents qualify prospective buyers before they show them properties. They determine how much cash the buyers have available for a down payment, and estimate the size of loan they'll be able to get.

Institutional lenders, such as banks, savings and loans, thrifts, and mortgage brokers use a formula to qualify borrowers, based on the buyers' income and monthly debts. If you are selling your home yourself, you'll want to learn how to qualify your buyers. (In chapter 14, you'll find a qualification worksheet, similar to those used by lenders.) It's a monumental waste of your time to accept an offer from someone who has no chance of getting a loan to buy your home.

Good Terms Can Increase Saleability

Another factor that can influence the saleability of a home is the availability of financial terms that can be offered to a buyer. When the real estate market in your community is healthy, when interest rates are low, and your home is readily financeable, you won't need to be concerned about providing special terms that make it easy to buy. But if, for any reason, buyers will have difficulty financing your home, or if the market is glutted with similar homes, you'll increase your chances of a profitable sale by offering attractive terms.

Better financial terms might mean an assumable loan, or perhaps your willingness to carry a contract or other seller financing. (Be sure to study the cautionary note about seller financing, later in this chapter.) "Terms" could mean that you, the seller, would be willing to pay some of the buyer's closing costs, such as discount points, so that the buyer is able to obtain a loan at an affordable interest rate. Terms can be valuable; a home with excellent terms will be worth more than one without, especially in a tough market.

Because of this, it is important for sellers to be knowledgeable about financing practices and costs. You'll find all the information you'll need in Chapter 14 of this book.

At Last... An Offer!

Finally that exciting moment comes, when a prospective buyer decides to make an offer to buy your home. If you're selling your home without an agent, your buyer may bring you a written offer, but more likely, you'll have to figure out how to get the details of the offer down on paper. While you and your buyer can sit down together and write out the terms of the offer on a sales agreement form from a local office supply store, there are so many legal points to consider and so much at stake, you would be well advised to let an attorney draw up the agreement. At the very least, have your attorney look over any offer you prepare yourself, **before** you sign it. Lawsuits are far too common in real estate transactions to leave yourself unprotected.

If you've been working with a real estate professional, your offer will be brought to you complete and finished. Depending upon tradition in your part of the country, the offer to purchase will be presented to you by either your listing agent or the selling agent. Sometimes, both agents may meet with you to explain the terms of the offer.

What you'll be shown is a document that goes by many different names. Depending upon the particular form used by the agent, it may be known as an **Offer** or **Contract to Purchase,** or a **Sales Agreement and Receipt for Earnest Money**. This document will contain all the terms and conditions of the offer to purchase your home. Included will be such items as the price that's being offered, the amount of earnest money, the amount of the down payment and the method of financing. The offer will specify when the transaction will be completed (the date of **closing** or **settlement**), and the date the buyer wishes to take possession of the home. The buyer may have added some special requests, such as additional items to be included in the purchase price, items such as appliances or draperies. Also, the buyer may request the right to have a special inspection, such as a structural inspection or a termite and dry rot inspection.

In most offers, you'll find a clause that specifies how much you, the seller, will be required to pay for repairs that the lender may require. Lenders can be remarkably fussy in their demands, so be sure that you are willing to pay the amount outlined in the offer.

Study the fine print carefully and do not allow yourself to be rushed into signing until you understand completely what you are being asked to do and to guarantee. Take time to see your attorney if you have any doubts or questions.

Earnest Money and Down Payment Explained

Now let's go back to the terms **down payment** and **earnest money**. You'll find them mentioned in the offer to purchase. The down payment is that part of the sales price the buyer agrees to pay in cash at the time the closing papers are signed. It's the part that will not be financed by a loan or a contract.

Earnest money is a small part of the buyer's down payment that's presented in advance, in the form of a note or a check with the offer, to show the buyers' good faith. The buyers are indicating that they are earnest in their intent to buy. The amount of earnest money commonly offered will vary with the price of the home and local practice in your community.

84

Your real estate agent can tell you what is customary.

One tip: if the earnest money is in the form of a promissory note, this note should be redeemed with cash or a check within a reasonable time. Avoid any earnest money note that is not redeemable until closing, since that really doesn't show good faith on the part of your buyer.

After you and your buyer have reached an agreement on the offer, this first payment— the earnest money— will be held in escrow by a neutral third party, such as an escrow company, or an attorney. It may also be held in the clients' trust account of one of the real estate firms, if both buyer and seller agree.

The earnest money will be included in your proceeds at closing time. But if the buyer backs out of the agreement and refuses to buy your home, after all the contingencies are removed, you may be entitled to receive all or at least part of the earnest money as compensation for taking your home off the market at the time you accepted the buyer's offer. Whether you receive this compensation depends upon the terms of both your listing agreement and the accepted offer.

Usually a clause in the sales agreement allows the buyers to get the earnest money back if they fail to qualify for a loan. That's why it's so important to know at the start whether your buyers **can** qualify for a loan. If you accept their offer, then take your home off the market, only to discover later that they can't qualify, you've lost a month or so of valuable market time.

Seller Disclosures About the Home

Often, we often hear people say "Let the buyer beware." But in real estate transactions today, it should be "Let the **seller** beware." In recent years, the courts have held sellers increasingly liable for representations they make on sales agreements, representations about the condition of the roof, or the furnace, for example. Check the offer carefully before you sign, to see just what you are guaranteeing. If you know of a defect in your home, disclose it **now**, to avoid serious legal troubles later. And the practice of selling a home "AS IS" may not protect you legally if you haven't specifically listed what you know to be wrong.

In some states, you may be required to sign a disclosure statement, listing the defects and problems you are aware of. If you have any questions about what you are asked to sign, or concerns about your liability, consult with your attorney before you sign.

The Fine Art of Negotiating

Offers routinely cause more than their fair share of difficulties. The problem is this: buyers are inclined to be a little nervous. This is a big investment for them, and they don't want to make an expensive mistake. So to be on the safe side, their first offer may very well be appallingly low. It's sort of a Wish List of their idea of a perfect deal. Now if instead, they offered you exactly what you asked for, the question would haunt them forever, "Could we have bought it at a lower price?" So they start on their terms, and hope you won't be terribly insulted.

Of course, you **are** insulted, and a trifle hurt that someone just doesn't see the true value of your home. But don't be upset; there is a constructive way to negotiate offers to your advantage. First, be calm and openminded as you listen to the offer. You'll be given a certain amount of time to consider it, so recognize that you probably aren't under pressure to give an immediate answer. Second, ask your agent to clarify any parts of the offer you aren't sure you understand. And third, concentrate on those portions of the offer you find acceptable. That may be everything but the price, or nothing except the closing date, but start with the positives.

Whenever you receive an offer, these are your options: you may accept it in its entirety, or you may reject it. If you choose to reject it, you may simply do nothing, and hope the buyer will make another offer. Or, you may reject this first offer and make a written **counter-offer** to the buyer. A counter-offer is merely another offer, one that you've changed to the terms that you find acceptable. If you do make a counter-offer, you are modifying the first offer and sending it back to the buyer for his or her approval. It is then up to the buyer to accept or reject the second document, your counter-offer. If this is accepted, then you have a legal agreement. If the buyer rejects it, you have no agreement and both the original offer and the counter-offer are dead.

I always recommend that if you don't like the original offer, make a counter-offer, even if its chances seem very bleak. Treat the first offer as if it were the only one you'll ever receive. Don't reject an offer in a huff; you may never again receive one as good. So take your offer and concentrate on what's **right** about it. Write a counter-offer and keep the deal alive. After all, you still have the two important elements of any negotiation process: a willing seller and a willing buyer.

Every Seller's Dream: Two Offers at Once

Sellers often wonder what to do if two offers are received at the same time. If one is a good offer and the other is not, there's no difficulty. If both are good, one offer can be accepted and the second can be accepted as a back-up offer only, provided that the second buyers are willing to wait in the wings for the first offer to fail.

But what are the ground rules if both offers need some improvement? Can a seller juggle the two and keep both going? No; the seller is on dangerous legal ground if counter-offers are given to more than one prospective buyer at a time. But here are two options: the seller may reject both offers, and suggest that the buyers submit better offers by a certain deadline. Or the seller may make a counter-offer to just one of the buyers.

Should You Agree to Seller Financing?

Seller financing has its appealing points. Instead of receiving cash for their entire equity at closing, sellers are often asked to accept payment on an installment basis— usually a smaller cash payment at closing, with the balance paid in specified installments. The advantage to sellers is that it can be an attractive investment at an excellent interest rate, if they have no immediate need of the cash. Homes and buyers that may not otherwise qualify for an institutional loan are able to obtain financing— and a quick sale. But seller financing is like a loaded gun. Handled carefully, it's safe to be around. With the wrong moves, it can be dangerous. Here's a sad, but true, case study of seller financing gone awry.

Case History: Chainsaws Ready?

Walter called in a question to my radio talk show, House Calls. Five months earlier, he had sold fifty acres of heavily forested land to a young couple who hoped to build their dream home there someday. The youngsters were waiting for an inheritance check to arrive; they had no cash at the moment, but their prospects seemed excellent. Because Walter was— under a crusty exterior— a bit of a romantic, he agreed to sell the property with no cash payment at closing, but quarterly payments over five years, at a very attractive interest rate. He drew up a simple contract which he and the buyers signed.

His first hint of trouble came three months later, when the first quarterly check failed to arrive. He tried to call the young couple's home number (in another state) and he found that it was no longer in service. Frankly worried by now, he drove out to the land. As he rounded the last bend in the road, he could see... nothing. No towering firs, no second-growth cedar. The "buyers" walked away with an instant six-figure income, leaving Walter with land that was stripped bare, of both trees and value.

Walter's tale is indeed a horror story, but I can assure you that it is only one of the many I've heard over the years. Frequent problems include payments that are not made on time, property that is damaged or destroyed before the buyer defaults, and foreclosure difficulties. On the other hand, one common complaint I hear is this: "I agreed to sell on a ten-year contract and they want to pay it off now, after just four years. I don't want the cash; I wanted the income!"

Does that mean that seller financing should be avoided? Not at all. But if you are considering "carrying paper", do it only with expert legal advice. There are different forms of seller financing and your attorney can advise which type will offer you the protection you need for a safe transaction.

Understand Your Closing Costs

Don't accept any offer unless you know fairly accurately what your closing costs will be. If the buyers are financing the home through a lender, their costs will be considerable. But sellers are apt to forget that they'll have their share of expenses, too. You'll find a closing costs chart for both buyers and sellers included in Chapter 14.

Whenever you receive an offer, your real estate agent should give you what's known as a **sellers' net proceeds sheet**. That will give you a good idea of what you will owe at closing, and what you can expect to receive.

Here's an idea of the charges you, a seller, might face at closing. First, you'll have to pay off your existing loan at closing, unless your buyer is assuming it, or you're selling your home on contract. And there will be the final month's interest to pay on that loan, with a possible prepayment penalty. (Here's a suggestion: you might ask your lender to waive this penalty; some do.) Next, any second mortgage loans or home improvement loans will probably have to be repaid. If you live in an area where title insurance is commonly provided, you may be asked to pay for such a policy for the buyers. There may be an attorney's fee, if an attorney represents you at closing. Depending upon the time of year you sell, you may have property taxes due. Add to that the real estate commission, some minor fees, such as the recording and escrow fees and, in some states, sales tax or transfer tax. So before you sign the sales agreement, be sure you know where you'll stand at closing time.

Countdown to Closing

Even after the offer has been accepted, there's still plenty of work to be done. Your real estate agent will take care of most of the planning for the closing. If you are working on your own, without an agent, you will have to oversee the progress of the paperwork. First, your buyer will have to obtain financing, unless you are selling the home on contract. (In that case, a visit to the attorney is essential, to have the contract written or reviewed.) If you have an agent, he or she will help your buyer find financing.

New loans take a long time to process, so be sure your buyer has committed (in the sales agreement) to apply for a loan within a reasonable time. After loan application, you can expect to wait at least four weeks before your buyer receives loan approval on a conventional loan. And if your buyer is seeking government financing, the wait could be longer— six to eight weeks, perhaps. During this time, you can see that the whole transaction is proceeding smoothly by keeping in frequent contact with your real estate agent to make sure your buyer has applied for the loan and everything is on schedule.

The Appraisal of Your Home

About two or three weeks after the loan application, you'll receive a call from an appraiser, asking for permission to look at your home. The appraiser's job is to verify to the lender (at the buyer's expense) that your home is worth its selling price and is good security for the loan. In order to prove this, the appraiser compares your property to similar properties that have sold recently, comparing size, condition, and price? If you researched the market carefully before you set your asking price, your home will easily pass the test.

The appraiser may recommend to the lender that certain repairs be made to your home before the loan is issued. These might be costly repairs, such as a new roof, or minor items, such as repairs to a handrail. It's difficult to predict just what a lender may require. Usually these repairs must be completed before any loan money is released. If the home isn't up to snuff and you refuse to pay for repairs you agreed to in the sales agreement, then your buyer may be entitled to back out of the deal and get the earnest money back. On the other hand, if you agree to make the necessary repairs, then your buyer must go through with the transaction, or forfeit the earnest money. Often the cost of repairs can be a point of negotiation between you and the buyer.

Wrapping Up the Transaction

Once the buyer receives a firm loan commitment from the lender and the repairs have been made to the lender's satisfaction, the paperwork for the sale of your home can be processed. The procedure of **closing,** or **settlement** will differ depending upon where you live. Traditions vary around the country. For example, if you live in the eastern part of the U.S., your closing may well be held at the lending institution that is providing the new loan. If you live in the West, your closing may take place at the office of a title insurance firm or escrow company. In some places, the parties sign papers in an attorney's office.

No matter what the specific practices, the paperwork for the closing and the necessary accounting, will be handled by a neutral third party. In some parts of the country, buyers, sellers and their attorneys meet with a representative from the lending institution to close the transaction. In other areas, buyers and sellers never meet. They sign the necessary documents in individual meetings with an escrow officer. Ask your real estate agent how, and where, closings are handled in your community.

Should an Attorney Represent You?

Sellers often ask if it's necessary to have an attorney represent them at closing. Here, too, tradition varies from state to state. While legal representation is often not mandatory, in many situations it's wise to seek the advice of an attorney before you sign. Here is what I recommend:

- If you're confused about any document you're asked to sign, at any stage in the process, from the listing agreement to the closing, seek legal advice before you sign.

- If you are entering into a seller-financing agreement of any type, it's wise to have your attorney draft the financing documents or review your documents before sign.

- If it's customary in your area to have an attorney present at closing (your real estate agent can tell you this), then do so.

In general, if you have any doubts, at any step in the process, see an attorney. The cost of resolving legal problems that can occur in a transaction will far outweigh the price of preventive consultation.

Title Insurance

Title insurance is something still unfamiliar to many sellers, although it's being used increasingly in most parts of the country. Title insurance is a policy that guarantees the title to a property. Disputes over the ownership of a piece of property are not unusual. Title insurance prevents you from being overwhelmed by the costs of such litigation. While it has been the practice for the buyer's attorney to research the chain of title to the property to prevent problems from occurring, a title insurance policy is a more effective way to insure that title is clear. As a seller, you will be asked to pay for title insurance to protect the buyer. The buyer pays for a lender's policy. The cost of such a policy varies with the selling price of the home.

At the Closing Table

The closing or settlement is the time when all of the final documents are signed by both buyer and seller. The buyers may have by far the larger stack of papers to sign, since they will be signing documents relating to the new loan or assumption, as well as those for the purchase of the home. You, the seller, will be signing the deed for the buyers, transferring ownership of the property to them. You'll also be signing papers acknowledging the final accounting. Don't hesitate to ask questions before you sign.

Your check for the proceeds of the sale will be delayed until the documents have been signed and recorded. If a lending institution is providing financing, the lender may require an extra day to verify the documentation also. The escrow officer or attorney handling the closing can tell you in advance how long it should be before you receive your money.

Now that your home is sold, it's time to begin your new life adventure. Part IV of this book deals with the other side of a real estate transaction—the buyer's perspective.

Part IV
BUY A HOME FOR
RETIREMENT

Part IV
BUY A HOME FOR RETIREMENT

The U.S. Census Bureau estimates that more than 75% of Americans over the age of 65 are homeowners. That's an impressive statistic! Chances are very good that there will be real estate in **your** retirement future.

By far the greatest number of retirees decide to remain in the same community where they have been living before retirement. Contrary to the stereotypical image of the sunseeking senior, it is estimated that fewer than ten percent of older Americans pull up their roots permanently and head for a new life in a different locale.

Whether you are considering a long-distance transfer or a move to a new home in your present community, Part IV will help you explore the real estate options that are available to you, make a wise decision and offer, then pay for your purchase with cash or appropriate financing.

12

Consider Your Purchasing Options

If you're considering a move to a new home, it's time to take a closer look at your choices in the housing market. The following pages outline the options that are available to you, their investment potential, advantages and disadvantages, plus tips on evaluating each.

SINGLE-FAMILY HOME

The single-family home is the most popular housing investment today, but it is not the right choice for every older American. Advantages include privacy, independence and the right to use your property as you wish (within legal limits, of course). Disadvantages include the inconvenience and expense of maintaining the home and grounds. Many single-family properties become far too difficult to care for as their owners age. (For two ways to overcome this disadvantage, see the section on ECHO housing and accessory apartments later in this chapter.) In some neighborhoods, loneliness can become a problem for homeowners living by themselves.

An aunt and uncle of mine, both in their eighties, recently bought their first single-family home, after a lifetime of apartment and condominium residency. They are having a wonderful time, redecorating, clearing out the garden and walking to the nearby shops. So far, maintenance is a delight, not a drawback!

Of all the real estate purchase options outlined in this chapter, single-family homes are the easiest to evaluate and finance. Purchased wisely, they are an excellent investment.

Some planned housing developments combine a few of the advantages of both single-family and condominium ownership. In them, you'll find a neighborhood association with mandatory fees assessed by a board of directors, recreation facilities, sometimes neighborhood security and other benefits. Unlike most condominiums, owners have greater freedom (but not total freedom) in choosing exterior paint colors and landscaping. Repairs and maintenance are paid for by individual owners. If you are considering buying a home in such a development, be sure to evaluate the restrictions and fees, as you would those of a condominium. You'll find suggestions for doing this in the section that follows.

CONDOMINIUM

For many older Americans, condo life is close to paradise. It offers them companionship through close neighborhood ties, the advantages of home ownership and yet freedom from the demands of maintaining a single family home. With a condominium, you own— individually— your personal living unit, but share joint ownership of the common areas with the other condominium owners. That means that ownership of the grounds, common stairwells and recreational facilities is shared. Maintenance of these common areas, including the exterior the building, is paid for through a condominium association fee, assessed by the association's board of directors and paid by the owners. If you prefer not to worry about grass cutting and roof repairs, yet you'd like the advantages of amenities such as a pool, exercise room or tennis courts, a condominium may be perfect for you.

How to Evaluate Condominium Developments

Not all condominium developments are created equal. This applies, of course, to the physical features you can easily see and evaluate. However there are some underlying differences that are not so easily recognized without careful scrutiny. To invest wisely, it is necessary to know exactly what you're getting.

Condominiums are often not as sound an investment as a single-family home. There are two reasons for this. In most real estate markets throughout the U.S., the average buyer prefers a single-family home; condominiums are neither as familiar nor as sought-after. In other communities, notably in resort areas, the condo market has been overdeveloped; there may be a glut of units available. Both of these market conditions will affect the resale value, especially in tough selling times. During a recession, the condominium market in many communities will be the first and hardest hit.

That is certainly not true in every location or with every development. Price range is not the deciding factor in resale value. Some condominium associations (in all price ranges) are exceptionally well run, and properties there are at a premium, no matter what overall market conditions are like.

When you evaluate a condominium, consider first the physical appearance of the grounds and the units for sale:

- Are the building exteriors and common areas well maintained?

- Does the development offer the amenities that you enjoy?

- Are there recreational facilities that you will never use? (After all, you'll be paying for them in your association fee and a development without them may have lower fees.)

- Are the living units well constructed, with good quality materials and fixtures? Is there adequate soundproofing?

- Does the floor plan suit your lifestyle?

- Is the location of the unit within the development a desirable one?

- Is the development itself well situated, with easy access to shops and community facilities?

- Does it offer a safe, secure living environment?

- Will you have sufficient privacy?

- Would you enjoy having the other residents as neighbors? (You may like the homogeneity of an adult community or prefer the company of families with children.)

Now it's time to look at the hidden factors that make some condominium developments more successful than others. Before you make an offer to purchase a unit, study two documents of public record: the association bylaws and the C.C.& R.s (covenants, conditions and restrictions), or ask your attorney to review them with you. Note especially any restrictions that may be placed on your use of the property. For example, are you permitted to park your motorhome in your driveway, or hang clothes to dry on the patio?

Your accountant can help you evaluate the financial soundness of the association, and you'll certainly want to track the costs of the association fees. Have there been unusually steep increases in the past or have the fees been raised gradually? If the association is weak financially, extreme fee increases may be necessary in the future to cover maintenance costs. Remember, as a condominium owner, your investment is only as sound as the association itself.

Learn what the owner-occupancy rate is— the percentage of owners, rather than renters, who live there. This will affect the financeability of your unit. Normally, condo loans are similar to those for single-family homes, if the owner-occupancy rate is satisfactory to the lender. Statistics have convinced lenders that developments with a high percentage of owners living in the units are better maintained and a sounder investment. Therefore, most conventional lenders today want to see at least a 75% owner-occupancy rate before they will finance with a minimum down payment. This may not matter to you, but it could certainly affect your resale value if buyers are required to come up with a 20% to 30% down payment in order to override the lender's concerns.

If the condominium development has been approved by one of the major secondary market investors (Fannie Mae or Freddie Mac), by HUD or by VA, financing will be easier and faster.

Before you make a commitment to buy, spend time talking to as many residents as you can. Find out if they are pleased with life in their community, or disturbed by problems you may not have noticed.

RETIREMENT COMMUNITY

The condominium you choose to purchase may very well be located in a retirement community. Many of these communities provide rental apartment units as well; and some developments offer co-operative ownership facilities. (A **co-op** differs from a condominium in that the entire property is owned by a corporation whose stockholders are the residents. Think of it as joint ownership of the whole, rather than individual ownership of a unit and shared ownership of the common areas.) Retirement communities usually offer extended services to residents, such as a group dining room serving meals, and a nursing station or infirmary.

There is often an entrance fee required before housing may be leased or purchased. As in the regular condominium association, homeowners are assessed monthly fees to pay for maintenance and services provided. Your research of the development should include those areas covered in the discussion of condominiums, plus an in-depth look at the assistance services offered and fees charged. Guidance from your own attorney and accountant is invaluable; a purchase in a retirement community can be a complex real estate transaction requiring professional advice.

DUPLEX OR MORE

A duplex or "double" can be an excellent investment that serves a dual purpose. Not only are you assured of having carefully selected neighbors close at hand, but you'll also receive a monthly income. The maintenance and property taxes will be greater than that for a single-family residence and you'll have to perfect your skills as a landlord (although for a fee, property management firms can lease the unit, collect rent and handle tenant problems).

Side-by-side doubles rather than upstairs-downstairs units are usually a better investment, because of their privacy and "user-friendly" outside access. When shopping, look for these features as well as excellent soundproofing. Don't purchase without careful evaluation of the costs involved in maintaining both units and the tax considerations of the rental income.

Financing is readily available for duplexes, triplexes and four-plexes if you plan to live in one of the units. (Non-owner occupied housing is always more difficult to finance.) Loans and lenders are similar to those for single-family homes.

MANUFACTURED HOUSING

Manufactured housing has made great strides in recent years, with units available now that are attractive and well built. Those permanently situated on a parcel of land can be financed together with the land through long-term loans similar to those on standard "stick-built" homes, although a larger down payment is usually required. Those manufactured homes which are not permenently sited or those on leased land, as well as older models, are often classified by tax assessors as "personal property" rather than "real property". Financing available on these units is shorter in term and not usually as attractive as financing for real property.

The value of manufactured housing, as an investment, varies widely. In its finest form, when almost indistinguishable in appearance from a standard home, it maintains its value well.

ECHO UNITS & ACCESSORY APARTMENTS

Manufactured housing is put to excellent use as **ECHO housing**. This acronym, for Elder Cottage Housing Opportunity, refers to modular units that can be purchased or leased and installed in back or at the side of a single-family home. This affordable unit allows elderly or disabled persons to live independently yet close to family or friends who can offer care and support.

Accessory apartments offer the same advantages of assisted independence. These are complete, self-contained apartment units constructed within a home, for the use of an elderly or disabled person, or for a caregiver. In this way, aging parents can be cared for by their offspring, without the necessity of sharing their living space. As another example, the apartment might be leased to a college student, giving an elderly owner a feeling of security in knowing that help is close by, if needed.

Many communities forbid the use of ECHO housing and the creation of accessory apartments through restrictive zoning laws and covenants. Gradually, however, some are relaxing their rigid rules and permitting homeowners to add these units. For free booklets explaining ECHO housing and accessory apartments in greater detail, see the Resource List on page 187.

Have You Considered Renting Your Next Home?

Maybe home ownership is not the answer to your housing needs. Certainly there are tax benefits available to you as an owner, but the disadvantages of being tied to one piece of property and having your cash investment tied up as well, often outweigh these. This is the time when professional financial advice makes good sense. You can easily compare everyday costs such as rent, loan payments, utilities, taxes and estimated maintenance expense, but it is often difficult to evaluate the overall, longterm effects of homeownership on your finances.

It sometimes makes good sense to rent temporarily, especially if you are planning a move to a new community. Remember, if you have sold a home and are planning to defer your capital gain by buying another, you don't have to rush into a decision. IRS allows you two years from the date of your sale to buy (or build and occupy) another home. Take advantage of this provision to allow yourself time to choose wisely.

Know Your Market Before You Buy

Sounds pretty elementary, doesn't it? Of course, you should be intimately acquainted with the real estate market in your new community before you buy a home. Yet buyers are often so anxious to settle in Shangri-la, they ignore the fact that rainy days occur there, too. (Or hurricanes, tornadoes, earthquakes and heatwaves.) I grew up in a large metropolitan area, where tourists rave about the cleanliness, the beauty and the safety. Anyone who **lives** there knows it's not at all like that! So be careful not to base your assumptions on a visitor's view.

If you can afford to live and rent in your prospective community for a full year before you purchase a home, you will be able to make an educated evaluation— and you'll be right there to find the hidden real estate bargains. Don't be convinced that housing prices are increasing at such a rapid pace, you'll miss the best deals if you don't act quickly. It occasionally happens, but in most real estate markets, you'll do better by biding your time and watching the rush for awhile from the sidelines.

How to Get to Know a Market

Whether you'll be living in a new home in your present community or moving to a new area, it will pay you to do plenty of research about real estate prices and practices there. If you are moving from an area of higher-priced homes, you may well view everything in the new town as a bargain. Avoid paying too high a price by familiarizing yourself with the town or city as a whole, the individual neighborhoods and the homes for sale within them. Here's how:

- Subscribe to a local newspaper and study the real estate section in each issue.

- Write to the Chamber of Commerce for facts and statistics about the community.

- Contact two or three real estate agents and ask them to send you detailed information about sample homes for sale. A computer printout of homes that have sold and those currently on the market, plus photos from a multiple listing book can be helpful in determining what your housing dollar will buy.

- Or ask an agent in your present community to refer you to an agent in the new location. Many real estate firms have national and international relocation services that will have an agent contact you and provide information at no cost to you.

Worksheet: Evaluate a New Community

The worksheet on the following pages allows you to record your observations of the neighborhoods you are considering. Photocopy it as needed, for use in comparing several different communities.

Evaluating a New Community

The Neighborhood

Name or location of neighborhood:_____

Overall appearance: _____

Price range of homes: $_____

Association fees: $_____

Property tax rate: _____

Other community taxes:_____

Deed restrictions: _____

Transportation

Travel time to:_____minutes

Travel time to:_____minutes

Local mass transit: ❐ bus ❐ train ❐ other_____

Distance to transit stop or station:_____

Frequency of transit service: _____

Distance to freeway or major route:_____

Distance to airport: _____

Availability of Community Services

❐ Police or Sheriff: _____

❐ Fire Department: _____

❐ Hospital/Doctor: _____

❐ Post Office: _____

❐ Water & sewer systems:_____

❐ Street lights: _____

❐ Telephone service:_____

❐ Garbage collection:_____

❐ Cable TV: _____

❐ Library: _____

❐ Church/House of worship:_____

❐ Grocery store: _____

❐ Shopping mall: _____

❐ Service station: _____

❐ Parks: _____

❐ Swimming pool: _____

❐ Golf course: _____

❐ Tennis courts: _____

❐ Other: _____

Possible Drawbacks

Any of the following located in or close enough to the neighborhood to affect property values negatively:

- ❑ Airport: _____
- ❑ Railway: _____
- ❑ Freeway: _____
- ❑ Commercial areas:_____
- ❑ Industrial areas: _____
- ❑ Undeveloped land:_____
- ❑ Landfill or dump: _____
- ❑ Sewage plant: _____
- ❑ Power lines: _____
- ❑ Floodplain: _____
- ❑ Poor air quality: _____
- ❑ Other: _____

Neighborhood Notes

How well does this neighborhood meet my needs and wants?

In the next chapter, you'll discover how to narrow down the choices even further, then make an offer to buy your new home.

13

Make an Offer to Buy

Seasoned buyers are not necessarily smart buyers. Experience helps, of course, but real estate practices are always changing. Methods you followed in previous home purchases and ideas you accepted in the past without question may not be relevant or accurate in today's transaction. To buy wisely, it is necessary to keep informed about the practices and pitfalls you'll encounter as you buy your next home.

This chapter will help you implement the decisions you have made— about the type of housing and location you'd prefer— and get you ready to make an offer to purchase your home.

Choosing and Working with an Agent

There is really no advantage in working **without** a real estate agent when you buy a home; for one thing, the cost of the commission is already built into the listing price of the home. This is often true on homes that are for sale by the owner, so working on your own will not be a cost-saver. On the other hand, there are plenty of advantages in working with a conscientious agent, from the easy access to information, to the professional assistance in preparing and negotiating the offer, and seeing that the closing takes place as scheduled. Chapter 10 has covered in detail the basics of choosing a real estate agent. Even though that chapter was written with the seller in mind, it offers valuable information for both buyers and sellers about what to look for in a real estate firm and agent.

Of particular importance to buyers is the question of **agency**; this is one facet of real estate practice that has changed considerably in recent years. Does the agent you are working with represent you, or does he or she actually represent the seller? Make it a point to ask the agent, if you haven't been told at the outset of your business relationship. Traditionally, most residential agents have been seller's agents; by law, they represent the seller, whether they have ever met the seller or not. They must be honest and forthright with you, but legally they represent the seller's interests, not yours. If the agent who writes a purchase offer for you is a seller's agent, he or she has a fiduciary responsibility to relate to the seller any comments you make. If you say, "I'm going to start with a low offer, but I'll pay the full price if I have to," a seller's agent is required to pass this information along to the seller. (And guess what price you'll end up paying!) Buyer's agents, on the other hand, represent you, rather than the seller. They have no legal obligation to pass on such comments to the seller, unless you instruct them to do so.

Why wouldn't every buyer choose to work with a buyer's agent? For two reasons: first, there are still relatively few of them in the residential market, although this number is growing, and second, you may prefer to continue working with the seller's agent who assisted you in the sale of your home, or an agent who prefers to work in the traditional manner. If you work with an agent who represents the seller, you can still expect to receive excellent service, but you must be careful to remember where the agent's primary loyalty lies.

What Should You Expect from Your Agent?

No matter whether you are working with a buyer's agent or a seller's agent, you have a right to expect your agent to be conscientious in handling the purchase. But sometimes expectations differ as to what that level of service should be. When you are selecting an agent, don't be hesitant to ask specific questions about how the agent will work with you. Are you a buyer who prefers to drive through the community first, armed with a list of homes to track down? Or would you prefer to have the agent schedule a full afternoon of showings for you? Are you in a hurry to find and buy a home, or are you idly looking at this point?

Personalities differ. That's why it is so important to choose an agent who is willing to work in a way you, too, like to work. If you like to investigate thoroughly every available home in the entire metropolitan area before making a decision, make sure your agent has the time and willingness to spend it with you. If you want an agent who will preview the properties and narrow down the list before showing it to you, make that absolutely clear from the start. Good communication is essential for a healthy business relationship. You expect it from your agent, and you should offer the same in return.

The Search for the Perfect Home

Once you've chosen an agent you feel comfortable working with, the pleasure of looking at homes can begin. If you have not already read chapter 11, which gives advice to sellers, do so now. I want you to be well armed to resist all of the guerilla tactics sellers will use to make their home absolutely irresistible to you. If you are to buy wisely, you'll have to resist the emotional appeal of a home filled with the aroma of fresh-baked bread. You'll have to look beyond the half-empty cupboards and recognize that there's actually far too little storage space for your needs. You'll have to be particularly observant and discerning to judge a home dispassionately.

Using the Home Evaluation Worksheet

Once you start looking at properties, confusion can easily set in. Did the home on Maple Street have a laundry room or not? Was there a dishwasher, or a breakfast nook? Or was that the home on Elm Avenue? Make it easy on yourself! Make several photocopies of the **Home Evaluation Worksheet** included in this chapter, and take a copy with you on a clipboard when you look at a home. You'll find room to record notes about all the details and dimensions you'll want to refer to later.

Only by following closely the real estate market in a neighborhood can you hope to become knowledgeable enough to recognize homes that are priced well and those that are priced too high. Your research should include information about homes that have sold in the neighborhood recently, and those that are currently being offered. Get into the habit of going to Open Houses each week, and following the real estate ads in the local paper. If your agent belongs to Multiple Listing service, he or she should be able to provide you with plenty of data about specific homes, and may be able to run a computer printout each day, showing new listings and new sales.

Once you have become an expert on transactions within the community, you'll be ready to jump in with an offer as soon as you see a good buy.

Home Evaluation Worksheet

Address:_____

Home is ❐ on market; ❐ sold

Current listing price: $_____

Previous listing price: $_____

First date listed: _____

If sold, date and sales price: $_____

Property taxes: $_____

Neighborhood or condo association fees: $_____

Existing financing: ❐ assumable; balance: $_____

    type:_____

Terms offered by seller:_____

Condition of surrounding property:_____

_____

Lot size:_____

Year home built:_____

Builder warranty in effect:_____

Exterior materials, condition:_____

Foundation type, condition:_____

Insulation:_____

Roof, gutters and chimney (type, age & condition):_____

_____

Windows, type:_____

Landscaping:_____

Fences:_____

Patio, deck, pool, etc:_____

Garage: ❐ attached ❐ detached ❐ automatic opener,

    number of cars:_____

Driveway: ❐ shared; surface:_____width:_____

Parking for motorhome, boat etc:_____

Other buildings (sheds, etc.):_____

Size of home (square footage):_____

Number of levels:_____

Number of bedrooms:_____

Number of bathrooms:_____

Includes: ❐ dining room ❐ den ❐ home office

    ❐ family room; other:_____

Make an Offer to Buy

Dimensions:
Living room: _____x_____
   Notes: ❐ fireplace:_____
_____

Dining room: _____x_____
   Notes: ❐ fireplace: _____
_____

Kitchen: _____x_____
   Built-in appliances:_____
   Other appliances included in sale:_____
   Notes:_____
_____

Den, library or family room: _____x_____
   Notes: ❐ fireplace: _____
Master bedroom:_____x_____
   Notes: ❐ attached bath:_____
_____

Bedroom #1: _____x_____
   Notes:_____
_____

Bedroom #2: _____x_____
   Notes:_____
_____

Bedroom #3: _____x_____
   Notes:_____
_____

Bathroom #1: _____x_____
   Notes:_____
_____

Bathroom #2: _____x_____
   Notes:_____
_____

Bathroom #3: _____x_____
   Notes:_____
_____

Laundry room: _____x_____
   Notes:_____
_____

Basement: _____x_____
   ❐ Finished; ❐ Unfinished_____
   Notes:_____
_____

Attic: _____x_____
    ❐ Finished; ❐ Unfinished_____
    Notes:_____

_____

Other: _____x_____
    Notes:_____

Storage area: _____x_____
    Notes:_____

_____

Appliances, window coverings or furniture included
    in purchase price:_____

_____

_____

Heating system (type, age, condition, cost): $_____

_____

Air conditioning (type, age condition):_____

_____

Electricity:____amps; 220-240 volt lines for major
    applicances?_____
Water: ❐ well, P.S.I. pressure: _____; or
         ❐ community system _____
         monthly cost: $_____
Water pressure: ❐ excellent; ❐ good; ❐ poor
Water heater (type, age, condition):_____
Sewage: ❐ septic tank, size: ❐ gallons_____
        ❐ cesspool_____
        ❐ community sewage system, cost: $_____
Defects noted by owner:_____

_____

Defects observed:_____

_____

Miscellaneous notes:_____

_____

_____

Comparable homes (address, listing/sold price):

_____

_____

_____

The Importance of a Home Inspection

A new trend that is growing rapidly is the use of home inspection services. I would never buy a home today without a complete inspection by a qualified inspection firm (unless I had watched the home being built for me). The chances of a serious hidden problem escaping the untrained eye are simply too great to be ignored. Several states have enacted legislation requiring sellers to sign disclosure statements; while you will be given a copy of this, don't rely on it when you make a decision to buy. The seller may be even less observant than a casual viewer.

The time to request the right to have an inspection made is when your agent is preparing the the offer to purchase. Be sure that your request is written into the offer, and make your offer contingent upon your approval of the results of that inspection. That way, you won't spend money on an inspection before the offer has been accepted, and if you don't approve of what has been discovered, you will not be held to the agreement.

A full home inspection should cost around $200 to $300, and should cover all accessible areas, inside and outside the house. It should include a wood-destroying organisms inspection. However, if you note any particularly severe problem, you may wish to have an additional, specialized inspection made of that area also (such as a roof inspection, or electrical inspection). It is important to check the inspector's credentials and to ask for references. Most inspection contracts limit the liability of the inspector to the amount of the fee paid. Of course, $300 doesn't provide much consolation if the inspector makes a serious mistake, but reputable firms do carry liability insurance.

Should You Have a Survey?

While a survey of some types of property can be expensive, it does provide you with the knowledge that you are getting exactly the parcel you assume you are buying. Without a survey, if you discover later that the neighbor's garage is on your land, you may find you've lost the ownership of that land through the laws of adverse possession. With a survey, you would know of the problem before closing; at that time, you could renegotiate the deal with the seller or back out of the agreement. As with a home inspection request, a survey should be requested in writing in the offer to purchase, and your offer should be made contingent upon your approval of the survey results.

Making an Offer to Buy

Chapter 11 outlined the provisions that appear in the **Sales Agreement and Receipt for Earnest Money,** otherwise known as an **Offer to Purchase.** Your agent (or your attorney, if you're not working with an agent) will prepare a written offer, according to your wishes. Buyers are often uncertain when it comes time to determining how much to offer. How can you determine what a fair price will be? If you have done your research thoroughly, you will know whether or not the asking price is reasonable. When you make your offer, allow some room for negotiation (unless the market is so hot that you'll be in direct competition with other offers). Avoid "take it or leave it" offers— once a seller is antagonized, the offer will rarely get "taken".

Recognize that real estate practices vary widely from region to region. If offers are customarily at close to full price in your previous city, don't assume that's the case in the new community. The same is true of earnest money; $500 may be adequate to show good faith in your last town, while $5000 may be the usual amount offered in this location. Your real estate agent can help you determine what is reasonable and expected.

Pay particular attention to the details of your offer. What, exactly, are you offering? Don't rush through the fine print; make sure that you understand each provision before you sign. Will the possession date allow you to make a smooth transition from your present home? Would you like the window coverings to be included in the purchase price? What about the appliances? Now is the time to be certain that you have included those details that are important to you. Take time to sleep on your decision if necessary; in most real estate markets, there is no pressure to rush an offer. Before you sign the offer, you may wish to have your attorney review it. Once the offer is signed and accepted, you will be bound by your agreement and will no doubt forfeit your earnest money if you back out of the deal.

The Offer is Accepted!

I hope by now that you have read chapter 11, since it deals with the process of offer and acceptance. Once the seller has accepted your offer, you can turn your attention to any contingencies you may have included, such as a request for a home inspection or a survey. Your agent will help you with these details and will see that the paperwork for your closing is prepared according to schedule.

Now it's time to take a closer look at how you'll be paying for your new home.

14

Finance Your Home

No matter which way their political and social opinions lean, when it comes to financing a home, the majority of older Americans follow a conservative approach. Indeed, plenty of older purchasers choose to pay cash for their home, rather than finance it. It feels more comfortable to them not to be indebted to a lender and tied to a monthly mortgage loan payment. According to the U.S. Census Bureau, over 80% of homeowners over the age of 65 are living in debt-free homes.

Should You Finance or Pay Cash?

If you're debating the issue of cash vs. financing to purchase a home, you will find mixed views on the subject. After studying both sides of the issue, you'll come to the conclusion that there is no one "right" answer to the question. What is best for you will depend upon several factors: the purchase price of the home, the value of your cash reserves, the amount of income you expect over the next few years, the other expenses you anticipate, the interest rate you'd pay on a mortgage loan, and the interest your money earns invested elsewhere. You will surely want to consider your present and future lifestyle, as well as your age, your health and the length of time you intend to remain in the home.

While I do not advocate risky loans for any buyer, nor a "mortgage-it-to-the-hilt" philosophy for most older borrowers, there are times when it does make sense to finance a home. This chapter will review the types of financing homebuyers may wish to consider and some financing issues that pertain specifically to the needs and requirements of many older borrowers.

An Argument in Favor of Financing

Remember that real estate is not a liquid investment. Before you tie up all your savings by paying cash for a home, consider this: it may be difficult to extract that money quickly when you need or want to spend it on other things. If you have read Part II of this book, you've discovered that converting your equity into cash is not always easy, fast or inexpensive. Unless you sell your home, you'll find that you are strictly limited in the amount of equity that you are able to convert. Other types of investments are certainly easier to cash in.

Finance When You Buy, Rather Than Later

If your goal is to finance your home with a relatively large loan, the financing you'll be offered when you purchase a home is usually more attractive (in both lending limits and tax deductibility) than that offered on a refinance basis. If you pay cash when you buy, but hope to finance later, as needed, you will be limited in the amount of cash you'll be able to recover when you do obtain a loan.

Don't Finance Simply for the Tax Deduction

The tax benefit in financing a home, notably the deductibility of the interest on your mortgage loan, is not necessarily an advantage; often it's a trade-off. You pay it, you deduct it. It becomes an advantage to you only if you have a better investment or use for your cash elsewhere. Don't spend thousands of dollars financing a home simply to obtain a tax deduction of questionable value to you.

If You Haven't Financed a Home Lately

Expect to notice some changes at the lending office if you haven't applied for a home mortgage loan in recent years. The decade of the 1980s was a period of upheaval for the mortgage loan industry. The high interest rates in the early years prompted the development of some very imaginative loans. Many of these creative flights of fancy were simply too unwieldy, too risky or redundant and have mercifully disappeared. Yet some of the new variations proved to be an asset to both homebuyers and lenders; loans such as the Adjustable-rate Mortgage Loan (known as the ARM) have a very practical use, even in today's market. So when you visit a lending office, you can expect to find several basic types of loans, with almost countless variations on each. This chapter will help you to evaluate the financing that will best suit your needs.

Where to Get a Loan

Home mortgage lenders come in all shapes and sizes. Today, you'll find loans offered by banks, savings & loans, thrifts, mortgage bankers and mortgage brokers. In cities, it has become customary for the larger lenders such as banks or S&Ls to separate their home mortgage lending departments from their regular banking facilities. So it is quite likely that your local bank branch will no longer be a source of home mortgage money. Your banker will direct you to a centralized mortgage department.

The number of **mortgage brokers** has grown dramatically in many areas. A mortgage broker acts as a matchmaker between borrowers and lenders. A broker can offer a wide range of loans from lenders in your state or in other parts of the country— a sophisticated form of one-stop shopping. There are advantages in working with a mortgage broker, as well as disadvantages, too. While you are able to compare a wide variety of loans, with different features and (to a limited extent) different requirements, you may end up with a loan from a lender in another city or state. If problems should occur, it's not as easy to go knocking on your lender's door, and once the loan transaction is completed, your matchmaker-broker steps out of the picture.

One advantage in working with a mortgage broker may be the ease in which your loan application can be switched from one lender to another if your loan is denied by the first. Often it is possible to avoid paying for a second appraisal and credit check, since the mortgage broker has, in most cases, ordered these directly and can send them to a second lender if needed.

Many borrowers feel more secure in dealing with a lending institution that funds its own loans. Yet in today's fast-moving world of finance, if Bank ABC gives you a loan, don't assume that you'll be dealing with Bank ABC for the next thirty years— or even the next thirty months. Lenders routinely sell their loans on the secondary market to free up funds. As a result, your loan may be sold to an investor in another part of the country, whether you approve or not. In some cases, your original lender will still service the loan; that is, you'll still continue to send your payment to the lender who gave you the loan. In other instances, you'll be asked to start sending your checks to Bank XYZ which has just purchased your loan.

How can you prevent this inconvenience? You can't. But you can certainly ask your loan officer, when you apply for a loan, what percentage of that institution's loans are "portfolioed"— in other words, kept, and what percentage are sold. That will give you an indication of where you'll stand.

A word of advice: If you should ever receive a notice asking you to begin sending your loan payments to a different company name and address, check with your original lender to make sure that the request is legitimate. In fact, your lender is required to notify you of any change. Since this is a common scam that many borrowers have fallen prey to, be suspicious and double check the instructions.

Choosing a Loan Officer

The right loan officer can make the whole borrowing experience a pleasure; an incompetent or inconsiderate loan officer can cost you the opportunity of receiving a loan. Avoid choosing your loan officer by chance. Allow plenty of time to search and interview. Real estate agents learn from experience which loan officers work conscientiously to see that transactions stay alive during the financing process, so it's a good idea to ask your agent for recommendations. Choosing the right loan officer is far more important than searching for a lender who offers a slightly lower interest rate.

Conventional vs Government Loans

Most lenders today offer a range of both **government loans** (that is, loans that are insured, guaranteed or funded by federal, state or local governments) and **conventional loans** (any loan that is not a government loan). Within both of these broad categories, you will find similar loan types, from traditional fixed-rate financing to adjustable-rate loans. The variety of loans offered today can be quite overwhelming.

Government loans sometimes offer advantages conventional loans do not. It's wise to look at both before you make a decision. Here is a brief summary of the types of government loans you may encounter, with advantages and disadvantages of each.

FHA LOANS

The Federal Housing Administration, within the U.S. Department of Housing and Urban Development (HUD), offers programs to insure home mortgage loans so that lenders can provide affordable financing with a small down payment. FHA loans are widely available from lending institutions; a real estate agent can easily direct you to lenders in your community.

There is a maximum limit on the size of FHA loan you may obtain. This limit varies widely and is based on the median price of housing in each community. With most FHA loans (except some special, subsidized loans), there is no income limit, but the borrower must be creditworthy and able to repay the loan. If you are a purchaser with a small down payment and are intending to buy a moderate-price home, duplex, triplex or fourplex, consider an FHA loan. However if you have a down payment of over 20% of the home's value, you'll be better off with a conventional loan. The cost of the mortgage insurance required on all FHA loans will be unnecessarily costly for you.

VA LOANS

The U.S. Department of Veterans Affairs runs a guaranteed-loan program available to qualified veterans. Like the FHA loan program, these loans are widely available from lending institutions in most communities. Ask a real estate agent to help you find a lender. VA loans are ideal for borrowers without a down payment as it is possible to finance up to the full value of the home. (On more expensive homes, a down payment is required.) Eligible veterans, regardless of the size of their down payment, should take the time to evaluate this outstanding program.

FmHA LOANS

The Farmers Home Administration (FmHA) offers two different loan programs. One, which is available directly from local FmHA offices only, provides subsidized loans for low-and very-low-income borrowers who wish to buy a modest home in a rural community. A newer FmHA guaranteed-loan program is available through designated lending institutions and offers loans to moderate-income borrowers. There are Farmers Home Administration offices throughout the U.S.; ask a telephone "Information" operator for the one nearest you.

STATE HOUSING AGENCY LOANS

Forty-nine states plus the District of Columbia offer excellent loans to moderate-income first-time homebuyers or those who have not owned a home within the last three years. (Buyers in Kansas will find similar programs offered by individual counties, rather than by the state government.) While many older Americans don't fit this category, a good many do. These loans are usually available through participating lenders, but details of the program and a list of lenders are available from the state government agency which oversees the program in your state. If you have difficulty locating the housing agency in your state government, contact the National Council of State Housing Agencies in Washington, D.C., at (202) 624-7710. You'll also find a complete list with phone numbers in another of my books, **First Home Buying Guide/Fourth Edition.**

OTHER GOVERNMENT LOANS

Loans are also available from some local government agencies, such as community development offices. These loans are usually for low- to moderate-income borrowers who have not been successful in obtaining a loan from another source.

Choose the Type of Loan That Fits Your Needs

Home mortgage loans today, whether from a conventional or government source, fall into two broad categories: **fixed-rate loans** and **adjustable-rate loans**. A fixed-rate loan has an interest rate, and monthly payments that never vary over the term of loan. On the other hand, an adjustable-rate loan has an interest rate that may be increased or decreased by the lender on a regular, specified schedule. Within these categories, you'll find a breathtaking number of variations.

Old Faithful: The Fixed-Rate Loan

Because of the stability of their interest rate (and hence, the predictability of their monthly payments), fixed-rate loans have long been the most popular way to finance a home. When interest rates are low to moderate and the borrower can afford the monthly payments, there is no better loan for long-term financing. If you plan to live in your home more than three or four years, take a good look at the fixed-rate loans offered by your lender.

Short or Long Term? The Choice is Yours

You'll find a choice of both 15- and 30-year fixed-rate loans (and the choice is offered on other loans too). If you choose the 15-year plan, your monthly payments will be slightly higher (usually 14% to 19% above those on the 30-year loans), but you'll save a full 15 years worth of interest. Add to that the benefit of the one-quarter to one-half of one percent lower rate of interest charged by most lenders on their 15-year fixed-rate loans and the savings really increase dramatically. On two $100,000 loans, for example, at 8.5% for the 30-year and 8% for the 15-year, you'd save a whopping $104,791. by choosing the 15-year plan.

If you're concerned about being committed to making the higher payments required on a 15-year loan, you can achieve similar results by choosing a 30-year loan and increasing the size of your monthly payments voluntarily. Most lenders allow this today but be sure to ask your loan officer or loan servicing department if you would be permitted to make larger payments without penalty.

Adjustable-Rate Loans May Surprise You

Don't automatically rule out adjustable-rate mortgage loans because they feel risky. You might be quite pleasantly surprised at the advantages they have to offer, benefits you can't find in fixed-rate loans.

When interest rates are high, adjustable-rate loans are popular. Since the interest rate charged by a lender on an ARM loan is lower than that on a fixed-rate loan. This, in turn, means that monthly payments for an ARM loan are lower than those for a similar-size fixed-rate loan. Lower payments make a loan easier to qualify for and easier to obtain.

Optimists choose ARM loans because they hope that interest rates will drop and, hence, their monthly payment will be lowered. But there are other reasons why you might find one perfect for your needs. One woman, who called a question into my talk show, House Calls, had never considered an ARM, yet it successfully solved her financing problem.

Case History: A Juggling Act

Anne, a widow, lived in the country home that she and her husband had shared. But she was anxious to head south, to the new retirement life she had planned in California. Her home was on the market, with plenty of activity, yet no offers so far. While she wanted to buy a condominium in California immediately, the cash that would be used to pay for the new home was tied up in her present property, which was free and clear. Both homes were roughly the same price. Should she try to refinance this home with a fixed-rate loan, take the cash and put it toward the sales price on the California condo, dipping into her cash reserves to make up the difference?

It didn't sound like a workable plan to me, for several reasons. If Anne were to move to California immediately, the condo would become her primary residence. She'd have a difficult time refinancing a home that she was leaving, especially one on the market. Moreover, refinances don't yield as much cash as purchase money loans. So I suggested that she finance the new condo, and— to her surprise— do it with an adjustable-rate loan.

Here's why: her home would sell, most likely within a few months, and at that time, Anne could take the cash from the sale and pay off the loan on the condo. So why should she pay six or eight months of higher interest by choosing a fixed-rate loan? Even if the home took a few years to sell, Anne would still be ahead with an adjustable-rate loan, since the interest savings would be that dramatic. Anne took my advice, her home sold within a few months and she's enjoying the California sunshine in a condo that's free and clear.

If You Like to Pay Down a Loan Quickly...

Adjustable-rate loans are excellent short-term financing, but they have another advantage that is unique: the monthly payment will be adjusted downward to reflect extra payments against the principal. In other words, if you sell your vacation home and apply $50,000 of the proceeds to the $150,000 principal balance on the adjustable-rate loan on your primary home, your monthly payment will be reduced when your interest rate is next adjusted. If you had chosen a fixed-rate loan your payment would remain unchanged, no matter how quickly you paid down the loan balance. Since the payments on an ARM are re-amortized when the rate is adjusted, you reap the full benefit of a lower loan balance.

To understand this feature, let's take a look at how an adjustable-loan works. All ARM loans have four factors in common:

- **Period of Adjustment**: How often the interest rate will be adjusted. For example, a "1-year ARM" has an adjustment period of one year, which means that its interest rate will be adjusted once a year. A "six-month ARM" will be adjusted every six months.

- **Note Rate:** The initial interest rate the lender will charge. The shorter the period of adjustment, the lower the interest rate. For example, you can expect the interest rate on a 5-year ARM to be close to that on a fixed-rate, while the interest rate on a one-year ARM might be 2% to 3% lower.

- **Index:** The guideline used as the basis for adjustment. If the index has increased at the time of adjustment, the interest rate on the ARM will be raised accordingly. Different loans will be based on different standard indexes, some being more volatile than others. An example of one index in use now is the one-year Treasury Bill discount rate.

- **Margin:** This amount is added to the index rate to establish the interest rate on an ARM. As an example let's take an ARM with a margin of 2.75%; if the index is at 4% at the time of adjustment, the interest rate will now be 6.75%.

The graph on the next page shows how the interest rate on an ARM is adjusted. Notice that fluctuations in the index only affect the ARM's rate at the time of adjustment.

Safety Features on an ARM

Today's ARMs have safety features that limit increases in interest rates (or decreases too, for that matter). The **lifetime cap** sets the maximum percentage of increase or decrease that may occur over the life of the loan, while the **adjustment cap** limits the amount of increase or decrease at each adjustment period. Even if your index hits an all-time high, your ARM loan will be limited by its caps.

Another feature to consider is a **convertibility** option. Some adjustable-rate loans offer the borrower the option of converting the ARM to a fixed-rate loan at some time during the term of the loan, at little expense. You may be charged a slightly higher interest rate for a convertible ARM and relatively few borrowers ever convert. Before you choose this option, be careful to note the times you will be allowed to exercise your option; some loans offer very limited opportunity for conversion.

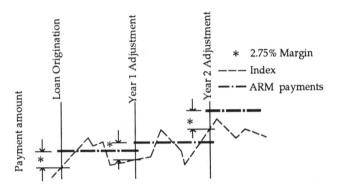

1-Year ARM with a 2.75% Margin

When you shop for an ARM, you have all of these variables to consider, so these loans are more difficult to compare than fixed-rate loans.

Other Loans You May Encounter

There are many other loans available on the market today. Loan fads are at least as prevalent as clothing fads. However, for most borrowers over the age of fifty, the two basic loans— fixed-rate and adjustable-rate— should meet most home-financing needs.

Stay away from any loan that is risky. In recent years, loans with balloons have been popular. (A **balloon** is a required lump-sum payment to repay the loan in full by a certain specified date, such as five or seven years into the term.) In spite of some safeguards on these loans, they are far too risky for most older Americans.

Any loan that seems too good to be true should be viewed with suspicion. If the enticing monthly payments you're permitted to make at first seem too low to cover the actual interest that is due, be sceptical. What you may be looking at is a loan with **deferred interest** or **negative amortization**; the interest you should have been paying gets added to your loan balance. After a few years, you may owe more than when you started! If any loan seems risky or if you're not sure of the best course to take, ask your accountant for advice.

Discount Points and Loan Fees

Comparing loans today is like comparing mangos to pineapples. It's not an easy job. Yet it does pay to comparison shop before you choose financing. One confusing feature to prospective borrowers is the fee charged by the lender to cover the basic cost of making the loan. This is usually called the **loan fee** or **loan origination fee** and is usually expressed as a percentage of the loan amount, often one or two percent.

Sometimes you'll find that the percentage quoted is higher than you might expect. Perhaps in this case, the lender has included the cost of **discount points** in the loan fee. Discount points are a form of prepaid interest, and by collecting this interest at closing, the lender can offer you a reduced interest rate. Each discount point costs you one percent of the loan amount. On a $100,000 loan, for example, each discount point will cost $1000. The choice of whether to purchase discount points or not is yours; if you want to lower the interest rate and reduce your monthly payments, you can choose a loan with discount points. Your accountant can offer sound advice on this matter.

While the discount points you pay when you buy a home are fully tax deductible in the year they are paid, those on most refinances are not, but may be deducted over the life of the loan. (See the refinancing tax tip in chapter 4.)

Assumptions and Assumability

In the good old days of lending, up to the late 70's, many or most loans were assumable. Sellers could allow buyers to take over their home mortgage payments and the lenders willingly accepted this. But when interest rates climbed sharply, lenders had second thoughts; all of a sudden, these valuable old low-interest loans were being passed from buyer to buyer and lenders were losing business.

Today very few fixed-rate loans are assumable. Those that are— mostly government loans— are no longer freely assumable, except by qualified buyers; there are restrictions that strictly limit the assumption process. Adjustable-rate loans are still often assumable, but lenders know that they'll likely be able to raise the rate if needed. The assumability of an ARM is not a particularly valuable feature.

Loan-to-Value Ratio

If you are willing and able to pay a sizeable down payment when you buy a home, you are considered by lenders to be a much better credit risk. Small down payments make them a little nervous, so much so that they require borrowers with less than a 20% down payment to pay a **mortgage insurance premium** to offer the lender protection should the borrower default. This can add considerably to your closing costs and monthly payments, so it's best to avoid it when possible.

To classify their loans according to risk factor, lenders consider the **loan-to-value ratio**: the size of the loan divided by the value of the home, expressed as a percentage. You'll often hear this referred to as the LTV or LVR. Loans with a small down payment will have a high LTV. For example, a $100,000 home with a $5,000 down payment will need a $95,000 loan— a 95% LTV loan. Borrowers seeking high LTV loans will not only required to pay mortgage insurance premiums but will also be required to jump extra-high hurdles when qualifying for the loan. You'll find these stricter requirements in the Qualification Worksheet later in this chapter.

Financing a Second Home

If you want to finance a second home— whether it's strictly a vacation home or one you hope to retire to— you'll find that the lending rules are very much more restrictive than those for your primary residence. While the types of loans themselves are similar, you will need a down payment of at least 20% of the purchase price. You will also be required to prove to the lender that you have sufficient cash reserves (in addition to your down payment) to afford a second home. These reserve requirements are usually higher than those for your principal residence.

When you apply for second-home financing, the loan payments on both residences will be used to determine your qualifying ratios.

If their primary home is free and clear, many owners find it easier to refinance it, then use the cash to buy a second home. Fewer lending hurdles to leap, but the drawback to this approach is that the lending limits on a cash-out "refi" are even lower than those on second-home financing.

How To Qualify For A Loan

In the past two decades, lending requirements have become stricter. Since institutional lenders expect to sell many of their loans to secondary market investors such as FannieMae, GinnieMae and Freddie-Mac, the loans that they offer conform to the lending guidelines set by these investors as well as by the providers of private mortgage insurance. If you are unable to qualify for a "conforming" loan, you may find a **non-conforming** loan offered by some lenders. Non-conforming loans (loans that do not conform to lending guidelines set by the major secondary-market investors) have less rigid requirements for both the borrower and the property, but are often at high interest rates. Shop carefully!

When you apply for a loan, your lender will base a decision on these factors:

- the stability of your income,
- your credit history, and
- your expected housing costs and other debt obligations.

Your age will not influence the decision. If you can prove that you are worthy of credit and are able to repay a loan according to the lender's standard requirements, you will receive the loan.

Rule of Thumb for Loan Qualification

Qualifying is done by means of two calculations, both of which compare your monthly income and debts. You must satisfy each of these requirements in order to receive a loan. Many lenders use the following percentages to determine loan eligibility:

- monthly housing costs (principal, interest, mortgage insurance, property taxes, association dues, plus homeowner's insurance) may not exceed 28% of the borrower's gross monthly income, **and**

- total monthly debts (all of the above plus car payments, other loan payments, credit card expenses, alimony etc.) may not exceed 36% of the borrower's gross monthly income.

If you have a small down payment (less than 10% of the sales price of the home, you'll face more stringent lending requirements. In that case, substitute 25% for the 28%, and 33% for the 36% in the rule of thumb.

Note that the income figures used are for **gross monthly income**, that is income before taxes or other deductions have been subtracted. Remember, too, that only regular, predictable income may be counted. That rules out many year-end bonuses unless they are predictable and guaranteed by the employer. Commissions or non-salary income may be used if you can show consistent earnings. Social Security and pension income will certainly be counted, however your loan officer may request documentation to show that your pension income is scheduled to continue.

Loan Qualification Worksheet

The following worksheet will help you calculate the approximate size of loan you'll be qualified to receive. While there is remarkable similarity in lending standards throughout the nation, rules do vary somewhat from loan to loan. You'll find that this worksheet is a good starting point; it will give you a good estimate of your borrowing power.

First you'll need to assemble some information. A quick call to a lending institution or your real estate agent should provide the necessary figures. Here's what you'll need:

What's the interest rate on new loans?

Find out what the current rate is on the type of loan you're interested in. Not sure yet which type? Try rates for both a fixed-rate loan and an ARM, to note the differences.

Will mortgage insurance be required?

If so, what will the monthly premium be? A loan officer can give you an approximate amount for this estimate.

What will the property taxes cost?

You'll need to have a rough idea of the monthly cost of property taxes for your new home. Your real estate agent can give you sample tax figures for homes in different neighborhoods. Pick one you think may be close to the type of home you'll buy. This is just an estimate and an discrepancy in the tax figure won't greatly affect the outcome.

What is the cost of homeowner's insurance?

Again, you'll just need a ballpark figure: how much is insurance likely to cost per month for your new home? Real estate agents often can quote approximate figures, based on past experience, or ask your insurance agent.

Use a calculator to help you estimate both of your qualifying ratios. Expect different results from each one; often the first ratio produces a much higher loan amount than the second. But which one will the lender use? Here are the guidelines:

QUALIFICATION WORKSHEET

Housing Cost Ratio:

A. Maximum Allowed For Housing Costs:
Gross monthly income: $_____

(multiply by .28)   x .28 *

Total: $_____

B. Total Monthly Housing Costs:
Monthly costs of:
    Property Taxes $_____
    Homeowner's Insurance   _____
    Mortgage Insurance   _____
    Association Fees   _____

Total: $_____

C. Maximum Allowed For Monthly Principal and Interest: $_____
(subtract "B" from "A")

D. Loan Data:
Interest rate   _____ %
Term of loan   _____ years

E. Amortization Factor: _____

F. Max. Loan Amount - Housing Cost Ratio: $_____
(divide "C" by "E" and move the
decimal point 3-places to the right)

Line "F" is the maximum loan amount determined by the Housing Cost Ratio.

* For 95% LTV Conventional Loans, use 0.25
For FHA loans, use 0.29

Total Debt Service Ratio:

G. Maximum Allowed For Housing Costs:
    plus Total Debts:
    Gross monthly income: $_____

    (multiply by .36)   x .36 *

    Total: $_____

H. Total Monthly Debts:
    Property Taxes $_____
    Homeowner's Insurance
    Mortgage Insurance   _____
    Association Fees   _____
    Car Payment   _____
    Other Loan Payments   _____
    Total Credit Card Payment   _____
    Alimony   _____
    Other monthly Payments   _____

    Total: $_____

I. Maximum Principal and Interest Pmts.: $_____
    (subtract "H" from "G")

J. Maximum Loan Amount - Debt
    Service Ratio: $_____
    (divide "I" by "E" and move the
    decimal point 3-places to the right)

Line "J" is the maximum loan amount determined by the Total Debt Service Ratio. Study the instructions preceeding
this worksheet to interpret the results of your calculations.

* For 95% LTV Conventional Loans, use 0.33
  For FHA loans, use 0.41

- If the maximum loan amount on the First Ratio exceeds that on the Second Ratio, the latter (smaller) amount will usually be your top borrowing limit.

- If the maximum loan amount on the Second Ratio exceeds that on the First Ratio, pat yourself on the back. Your total debts are low. In this case, the lender may possibly increase your First Ratio percentage to 30% or even 32% and the new First Ratio figure will be used as your maximum loan amount.

Timetable for Obtaining a Loan

Expect a conventional loan to take four to six weeks from the date of your loan application (the "loan app") to the date of closing. If the real estate market is in a frenzy in your community, it could take even longer. Government loans may take slightly longer than conventional loans to process, so allow about six to eight weeks for these.

When you have an accepted offer to buy a home, it's time to make formal application for the loan. (Many lenders also offer a pre-approval process to prospective buyers, checking credit-worthiness early so that a buyer is sure of having financing waiting before making an offer.) Call for an appointment with your loan officer and ask what information you'll need to bring with you. Most lenders can send you a list, and by having the various addresses and bank account numbers with you, the lending process will be considerably faster. At the time of your loan application, you'll be expected to pay for your credit report and the appraisal, so bring your checkbook.

Your real estate agent should have given you an estimate of your closing costs when you made an offer to purchase the home. Once you have chosen your financing, your loan officer will be able to give you a more accurate list of the costs associated with your new loan. Since many of these costs vary, depending upon the actual date of closing, the numbers you'll find on your final settlement documents will be somewhat different. (See the chart of closing costs for buyers & sellers at the end of this chapter.)

Speeding Up the Process

By staying in touch with your loan officer during the course of the verification process, you'll know that everything's on schedule. You can expect the credit report and verification letters from employers and banks to take two to three weeks. There may be errors in your credit report or questions about pension benefits or other income that will have to be cleared up and this can take a little extra time. The appraisal of the home should be carried out within two to three weeks also and your real estate agent should let you know if the appraiser has not yet appeared.

If title insurance will be purchased, you'll receive a copy of the preliminary title policy within the first two weeks. Read it and check it carefully for accuracy.

Locking the Interest Rate

Sometime between loan application and closing, the interest rate you'll receive on your loan will be "locked in", or guaranteed. Lenders' policies on rate locks vary widely. Some automatically lock the rate at the time of loan application, based on that day's interest rate for your type of loan. Others allow the rate to "float" until you ask to have it locked. Rate locks have a time limit (often 30 to 60 days), so be sure to ask about your lender's policy.

At Last... Loan Approval!

When your lender has gathered all the necessary information, credit reports and verification statements of your assets and income, your application will be submitted to the lending institution's underwriters for approval. You'll receive one of three answers: your loan may be approved, conditionally approved (that is, approved if a certain debt is paid off or income verified further), or denied. If your loan is denied but you can show additional information of your credit ability, your loan officer may re-submit the application for consideration. It's far better, though to present your strongest case right from the start.

Once your loan has been approved, it will usually take only a few days for an escrow officer to prepare the final documents for you to sign.

Ask to See Sample Documents

The papers you'll be expected to sign at closing are complex legal documents with plenty of small print. I'm always amazed at the number of borrowers who sign them without reading them thoroughly. If you'd like to arrive at the closing table well prepared, ask your loan officer for copies of the standard forms that you will be asked to sign. The figures won't be filled in— that must be done at the last moment— but you'll have an opportunity to study the fine print and ask for clarification if you don't understand a point.

Closing Costs for Buyers and Sellers

The following table shows the types of fees that both buyers and sellers can expect to pay:

CLOSING COSTS	Conventional Loan	Conventional Refinance	FHA Loan	VA Loan	Seller Financing	Cash Purchase / Sale	Estimated Closing Costs
BUYER'S USUAL COSTS							
Appraisal Fee	✔	✔	✔	✔			
Credit Report	✔	✔	✔	✔			
Loan Fee / Assumption Fee	✔	✔	✔	✔			
VA Funding Fee				✔			
Discount Points	●	●	✔	✔			
Buydown Fee	●	●	●	●			
Mortgage Insurance Premium	●	●	✔				
Underwriting Fee	✔	✔	✔	✔			
Document Preparation Fee	●	●	●	●			
Tax Service Fee	✔	✔	S	S			
Flood Hazard Report	✔	✔	✔	✔			
Survey Fee	●	●	●	●			
Re-inspection Fee	●	●	●	●			
Mortgagee's Title Insurance	✔	✔	✔	✔			
Excise Tax *	✔		✔	✔	✔	✔	
Interest Payment	✔	✔	✔	✔			
Down Payment	✔		✔	●	✔		
Homeowner's Insurance	✔	✔	✔	✔	✔		
Tax Reserves	●	●	✔	✔	●		
COSTS: BUYERS and/or SELLERS							
Tax Prorates	✔	✔	✔	✔	✔	✔	
Escrow Fee	✔	✔	✔	S	✔	✔	
Recording Fees	✔	✔	✔	✔	✔	✔	
Sales Tax *	✔	✔	✔	✔	✔	✔	
Transfer Tax *	✔		✔	✔	✔	✔	
SELLER'S USUAL COSTS							
Owner's Title Insurance Policy	✔	✔	✔	✔	✔	✔	
Reconveyance Fee	✔	✔	✔	✔		✔	
Real Estate Commission	✔		✔	✔	✔	✔	

* Where applicable   ✔ Fee usually charged
S Seller pays entire fee   ● Fee sometimes charged

Part V
TAX
CONSIDERATIONS

Part V
TAX
CONSIDERATIONS

The tax considerations of home ownership become of greater importance to us as we grow older. There are two reasons for this: first, there are tax benefits that apply only to older Americans and second, by the time retirement age arrives, many longtime homeowners have built up a sizeable tax liability in their home's increase in value. How to calculate the capital gain and, even more important, how to manage that gain to lower the tax bite are of great concern to many.

Other factors may also play a part in this later-life focus on tax matters: some homeowners are faced with the double whammy of a declining (or at least, not sufficiently increasing) income and rising property taxes. Then too, estate-planning raises tax questions that may affect decisions about a home.

This section of the book will address all of these tax considerations that are of direct concern to older Americans and their homes.

15

The Deductibility of Home Mortgage Interest

One of the pleasant side benefits of home owner-ship is the income tax deductibility of the interest you pay on your home mortgage loans. So far, that advantage has been considered by Congress to be **relatively** sacred, although not entirely so. When the 1986 Tax Reform Act (and subsequent tax rules) reduced, then eliminated the deduction of interest on personal debt, attention turned to home mort-gage loans as a handy source of interest-deductible money. Why not mortgage your home to the hilt, then use all that borrowed cash to finance a new car, a European jaunt or a diamond ring? If you're sitting on a hefty amount of equity in your home, like many older Americans, it may seem a good idea to do so. But before you rush to the lending office, consider carefully the tax implications of a refinance or an equity loan.

The same 1986 Tax Reform Act and other tax rules that wiped out the deductibility of interest on per-sonal debt also dared to invade the sacred area of home mortgage interest. In the good old, pre-1986 days, interest was deductible—period. Since that time, the rules concerning home mortgage interest have become considerably more complex. The com-plications increase when homeowners refinance or obtain an equity loan, a situation familiar to many older homeowners who've owned a home for several years. Further questions arise when homes are remodelled or updated. While the interest on the majority of home mortgage loans is still tax deductible, don't automatically assume that it is. After you refinance your home or take out an equity loan, you may be in for an unpleasant surprise at tax time.

Which Interest is Deductible?

The rule is this: You may deduct any interest you pay on up to $1 million of "acquisition debt", that is, loans secured by your principal residence (and also a second home) for the purpose of buying, building or substantially improving it. If, however, on October 13, 1987, the balance due on your mortgage loans for your primary and second homes was greater than your actual debt to buy, build or substantially improve the property, you may count the higher figure as "acquisition debt". As your loans are gradually repaid, your acquisition debt declines and may be increased only by substantial renovations.

In addition to this, you may deduct up to $100,000 of "home equity debt": debt incurred through refinancing, a home equity loan or line of credit secured by the property. There are some specific limitations and requirements that add further complexity to the rule. (For example, if you use the borrowed funds to buy tax-exempt bonds or single-premium life insurance, the interest is not deductible.) An accountant's advice is an excellent investment whenever you're thinking of borrowing.

Case History: A Matter of Interest

Since 1972, John and Emma Dunbar had been enjoying life in the family home they bought for

$65,000, with a $10,000 down payment and a $55,000 loan. Each year, on their federal income tax return, they received a deduction for the amount of interest they had paid.

Twenty years later, interest rates were appealingly low and the Dunbars decided to refinance. By this time, the original $55,000 loan balance was down to a mere $6,500 and the home was now worth $195,000. John and Emma used $15,000 of the borrowed funds to remodel the house, turning a large bedroom into home gym, spa and extra bathroom. Since they and their home both qualified for a larger loan, they opted to borrow $130,000. The additional money would pay off some personal debts, buy two new cars and an unforgettable anniversary trip to Tahiti.

Can the Dunbars deduct their entire amount of interest they'll pay on their new loan? No, not quite; here's why: By the time they refinanced, their original acquisition debt was down to $6,500. Since $15,000 of the new funds paid for the "substantial improvements", this could be added to their acquisition debt, to bring their total to $21,500. This is well under the one million dollar figure set by Congress, so the interest on this portion is fully tax deductible.

Now for the balance of the loan: $130,000 less the $21,500 "acquisition debt" leaves $108,500 in so-called "home equity debt". Since this is above the $100,000 ceiling allowed by the tax rules, interest on the $8,500 balance is not tax deductible. Fortunately for the Dunbars, the amount was relatively small but because of its non-deductability, proved to be a good deal more expensive than the Dunbars had expected.

So the moral of the story is this: Be sure to check with your tax accountant whenever you refinance your home or get an equity loan. The calculations for acquisition debt vs equity debt are not always clear-cut, so a second opinion from a professional source can save you money at income tax time.

16

Capital Gains Tax Tips

When you sell your home, you will be taxed according to the amount of **capital gain** you have realized in the transaction. Since 1986, there has been no specific rate for capital gain. Instead it is taxed at the same rate as your other income, to a maximum of 28%.

Those of you who have owned a home for many years are quite likely to have seen it increase in value considerably. And while you may now be living in a veritable goldmine, be assured that IRS is waiting patiently in the wings to collect a goodly portion of that profit in the form of the tax on your capital gain once you sell. So the challenge is to be aware of provisions in the tax law that will help you:

- reduce the capital gain and hence, reduce your tax,

- defer the tax on your capital gain, or

- legally wipe the slate clean of capital gain and avoid paying the tax on all or part of your gain.

While tax law changes in the mid-eighties were tough on many forms of real estate, your own home remains an excellent tax shelter— **if** you know how to take advantage of the loopholes Congress has left open to you. But the tax laws are complex; with such a great deal of money at stake, you are well advised to consult a tax accountant **before** you put your home on the market. I am surprised and dismayed by many of the questions that have been asked of accountants who were guests on my radio talk show, House Calls. These callers had sold their homes and suddenly discovered that the tax on their gain was far, far greater than anticipated. What loophole should they use? Unfortunately, **after** the sale is no time to plan a tax strategy; the most an accountant can do then is to try to minimalize the damage, and that's not easy. Because those callers misunderstood the law as it relates to capital gains and proceeded with the sale of a home without competent tax advice, there usually was little help that could be given after the fact. They paid unnecessarily high taxes that could legally have been avoided.

Calculating Your Capital Gain

Before you can decide which tax strategy to follow, you must determine the amount of gain you've realized in your present home. If you have owned previous homes, you may have "roll-over" deferred gain from these sales.

The following worksheets offer a three-step method to calculate your capital gains.

CAPITAL GAIN WORKSHEET

STEP I: Calculating Your Cost Basis

To determine your capital gain, you must first calculate what is known as your **adjusted basis**. Here's how to do it:

Add these figures:
the price you paid for your home $_____

plus: certain expenses incurred when you
purchased it such as: attorney fees   _____

appraisal fees: _____

inspection fees: _____

title search fees: _____

title insurance premiums: _____

recording fees: _____

transfer taxes: _____

plus: the price of any **improvements** you made
        to it (not **maintenance** costs, however)   _____

plus the cost of certain local government assess-
        ments that increase the value of your home: _____

Sub-total: _____

Subtract from this: the amount of gain you
        rolled over from a previous home: _____

Subtract also: any casualty loss incurred
        (damage or destruction from an event
        such as an earthquake, flood or riot etc.)   _____

Your adjusted basis: $_____

So far the calculations haven't been too difficult, especially if you've kept careful records of improvements or losses over the years. However the difficulty lies in knowing how to interpret the IRS' definition of the terms. If you re-roof your home or replace the cracked front walk, is this considered "an improvement" or "maintenance"? Tax rules allow improvements to be counted, while costs cannot. You'll find there are many grey areas that have been interpreted in previous tax decisions. Your accountant can advise what is, or is not, acceptable in your case.

There are other items that may or may not be used to increase your cost basis, depending upon the details of your particular situation:

- Did you enter into a lease-option agreement to purchase the home? The option fee and a portion of the rent you paid may be applicable to your cost basis.

- When you bought your home, did you pay any expenses incurred by the seller? (For instance, you may have agreed to pay two years' worth of overdue property taxes for a seller who was unable to do so.)

- Has your local government assessed your property for certain benefits that may have improved the value of your home? (For example, in one neighborhood, homeowners received assessments for replacing a gravel road with a paved street and sidewalks.)

If any of these items pertain to your home, be sure to ask your accountant how they might be used to increase your cost basis.

STEP II: Calculating Your Adjusted Sales Price

This figure is the amount that you realize from the sale of your home. Here is how to calculate it:

From the actual selling price of your home: $_____

Subtract your selling costs, such as:

    real estate commission: _____

    closing costs: _____

    advertising fees: _____

    legal fees: _____

    inspection fees: _____

    buydown fees or discount points paid for
    buyer (but again, no repairs or maintenance):_____

Your Adjusted Sales Price: $_____

STEP III: Calculate Your Capital Gain

    Your Adjusted Sales Price (from STEP II): $_____

    Minus your Adjusted Cost Basis (STEP I):   _____

    Your Capital Gain: $_____

Deferring Capital Gains

When the 1986 Tax Bill erased many of the loopholes that had previously lightened the tax burden on real estate, it left intact the provision allowing Americans to defer the gain realized on the sale of their home by rolling it over into the cost basis of the new home. If you've been buying and selling homes over the years, you're no doubt accustomed to this benefit. However, for those who have not sold a home recently, here are the highlights of the provision.

When you sell your principal residence, you may defer the tax on your capital gain if, within two years before or after the sale, you buy (or build and occupy) another home that costs at least as much as your home sold for. That gain becomes a part of the adjusted cost basis on your new home. By rolling over your capital gain each time you sell and move to a more expensive home, you can defer the tax almost indefinitely.

There are some points to note about this provision, however. IRS counts that two-year period to the day and will not permit an extension. And while you **do** have to buy a more expensive home to defer the tax, you **do not** have to use all of your cash proceeds from the sale as a down payment. You are permitted to finance the new home with as large a loan and as small a down payment as you like, thereby saving your cash for other purposes. The rollover provision may be used no more than once every two years, with some exceptions, such as certain job-related moves.

If you have had an office or a rental unit in your home, for which you have taken a tax deduction, you will not be permitted to roll over the entire capital gain. If, for example, your home office or apartment counted as 15% of the total house, then you may roll over only 85% of your capital gain.

Not Buying a Higher-Priced Home?

If you are considering buying a home with a price tag that is not higher than the sales price of the home you are selling, (or if you are not intending to buy a home at all) be aware that you will be taxed on your capital gain. However, work with your accountant **before** you make an offer on a lower-priced home, to discover how to minimize your tax liability. For example, you may be permitted, in this situation only, to count spruce-up costs on your old home as sales costs. Your accountant may also help you find ways to "increase" the new home's price through capital improvements. For example, if you sell a home worth $100,000 and purchase a $90,000 home, IRS will allow you to add $10,000 worth of improvements to the new house. If this is done within 24 months of closing, the capital gain on your previous home may be deferred. But all of this should be planned before the transaction.

While every homeowner, regardless of age, is permitted to defer the tax on capital gains with a roll-over, those 55 years of age and older have another option open to them: a one-time $125,000 capital gain exclusion. So when you reach that age and are evaluating the pros and cons of using your one-time $125,000 capital gain exclusion, it is important that you understand the other choices that are open to you when you want to lower your tax bill. Deferring your gain through a roll-over is just such an option.

The $125,000 Capital Gains Exclusion

By the time they've reached their mid-fifties, many Americans have accumulated quite a sizeable profit on a single home or rolled-over gains from a string of sales. Now they may be ready to "downsize" and move into a smaller house. The tax consequences of the purchase of a less expensive home could be quite a blow. The $125,000 exclusion comes at just the right time.

This exclusion allows homeowners 55 years of age and older to shelter from tax up to $125,000 of the profit from the sale of their home. But there are some specific rules relating to this:

- The $125,000 exclusion applies to a married couple who file joint income tax returns and also to a single person. A married couple who file separate returns are limited to an exclusion of $62,500 for each spouse.

- Although it is not necessary that you be living in the home at the time you sell it, you must have lived there for at least three of the five years before the sale. You are permitted to rent the home or leave it unoccupied as long as you've met the three year out of five rule.

- If you and your spouse own the home jointly, only one of you must meet all three requirements.

- If you marry a spouse who has previously used his or her exclusion, either as a single person or in an earlier marriage, neither of you will be permitted an exclusion after you marry.

- If your profit is less that $125,000 and you don't need to exclude the total amount allowed, you will not be permitted to tuck some aside for the next sale. This is a one-time exclusion, whether you shelter $20,000 or the full $125,000.

- If you have a rental unit (such as an accessory apartment) in your home, you may not exclude the gain on that portion of the home.

Because of these rules, and especially the last one, sellers 55 years and older are often faced with a dilemma: is this the sale in which to use the exclusion? Or will the next house show an even greater profit? If you are not able to shelter the full $125,000 gain, or even close to it, and you are buying another home, it may be wiser to wait to exclude the gain on the next sale. If the new house is lower in price than the one you are selling, your accountant can help you estimate your tax liability with and without the exclusion, on this and your next home.

Some homeowners express concern that if they don't use the exclusion now, and die before taking advantage of it, their heirs will be faced with a much larger capital gain tax burden on all that profit. Absolutely not! When a homeowner dies, the tax on all the capital gain in his or her home is excused. The purpose of the exclusion is to allow older Americans to cash in on their investment and keep the profit their home has earned. If, instead, they choose to remain in their home and not take advantage of the exclusion, their profit is not forfeited, but simply remains invested in the property.

One variable remains, in our discussion of capital gains, and that is the changeability of the tax laws. They are certainly not carved in stone but are amended freqently. The taxation of capital gains is an issue that is brought up regularly on Capitol Hill. We do not know, from year to year, how our profit will be taxed. Can anyone predict what Congress will do? Keep in mind, though that a majority of voters are homeowners and an even greater majority of Americans over the age of 55 own a home, close to 75%, in fact. That's why tax provisions benefiting homeowners are usually slow to be taken away.

17

Charitable Gifts of Real Estate

In the fast-paced world we live in, families don't stay put. Rarely today do we hear of a family remaining in one home for generation after generation; most of us move several times in our adult life. The "ancestral home" is far more likely to be found in a gothic novel than in any American true-life story.

Chances are good that your offspring will have no desire to move in to your home when you vacate it. They'll have homes and a life of their own. So that means that your property will be sold, either during your lifetime or after your death.

Consider a Charitable Donation of Real Estate

If you have considered making a sizeable donation to a charitable institution, consider giving a gift of real estate instead of cash. This can be surprisingly advantageous for both you and the institution— in fact, far better for you, in most cases, than selling the property first and donating the proceeds to charity.

There are many ways to structure the gift, depending upon your needs and the type of property involved. Benefits to you, the donor, may include an immediate tax deduction, avoidance of capital gains tax, the opportunity to remain in your home as long as you wish, or a lifetime income. The benefits you'd like to receive will determine the type of agreement you'll wish to make.

Be advised that the contracts and tax issues involved are complicated and should be undertaken **only** with the assistance of your attorney and your tax advisor. Laws pertaining to charitable gifts and trusts vary from state to state, and tax laws are revised frequently. So it is very important that you seek good professional advice before you proceed.

There are different types of charitable donations that apply to real estate. In this chapter, we'll take a look at those most commonly used by private individuals.

Types of Gift Property

Any real estate that you own can be given as a charitable donation. This includes your own home or vacation home, residential or commercial rental property, a farm, timber land or other undeveloped acreage.

Outright Gifts of Real Estate

If the gift property is not a home that you'll be living in or land that you want to continue using for any purpose, you can give it (with no strings attached) to a charitable institution in return for an immediate tax deduction. In this case, you will avoid paying tax on your capital gain and you will receive an income tax deduction based on the appreciated value of the donated property.

Compare this to the smaller tax benefit you will receive if you sell the property first, then give the entire proceeds of the sale to the charitable institution. In that case— by selling the property and giving cash— you can claim a similar tax deduction for the value of your gift but you will be taxed on the capital gain (unless it is excluded under the rules outlined in Chapter 16.) So it can be far more advantageous to donate the property itself.

An exception to this rule is for rental property that has depreciated in value, giving you a capital loss. By selling the property first, you will be able to claim your loss on your federal income tax return, then take the deduction for the gift of the cash proceeds.

But I'd Like to Keep Using the Property

Sometimes an outright gift is not feasible, especially a gift of your own personal residence. Yet there is a way to make your donation today and receive an immediate tax deduction, while continuing to enjoy some of the benefits you realized as owner.

It is possible for a person to give real estate to a charitable organization while retaining the use of the property during his or her lifetime or the lifetime of both a husband and wife. There are many different forms of Charitable Remainder Trusts, but they can be classified in two broad categories, depending upon whether the property involved is your own residence or not. The benefits you'll receive, in addition to your tax deduction, will be quite different for each.

When the Gift is Your Home

Unless you are making an outright gift of your home and are moving out immediately, you'll want to structure an agreement that will allow you to continue living in your home. In this case, you will deed the house to the charitable institution, while retaining what is known as a "life estate". You may take a tax deduction in the year the deed is signed, but you can go on living in the home, paying your property taxes, cutting the grass, repairing the roof and taking care of all the normal maintenance costs. When you die the life estate is terminated and the charitable organization gains the full use of the property, including the right to sell it. If you should decide to move out of your home, you can make a gift of the life estate to the charity at that time.

The tax deduction you'll receive when you retain a life estate may be smaller than that for an outright gift, since this agreement has a few strings attached. The size of deduction is determined by the value of the home minus the value of the life estate you retain. The market value of your home is easy to determine by means of a fee appraisal. The value of the life estate will depend upon your age at the time you make the gift.

When the Gift is Not Your Home

The gift of property other than your own residence can reap an additional benefit in the form of an annuity income for you, the donor. Let's use as an example your vacation home on Maui (although it could just as easily be farmland in Nebraska or a commercial building in Detroit). If you were to make a gift of your vacation home to a charitable institution, the home could be sold by the institution and the proceeds invested to provide a lifetime annuity income for you. The amount of the income would be determined by the value of the property; it is reasonable to expect an annual income of 6% to 8% of that value. Some institutions are entitled to underwrite their own annuities; others use life insurance annuities to provide income to donors.

Again, the tax deduction you'll receive is less than that for an outright gift of the property without an annuity. An IRS formula is used to determine the allowable deduction.

Types of Institutions

Charitable organizations differ in their gift tax status and this can affect the size of your tax deduction. So it is important to be aware of these differences before you consider making a gift to a particular charity. Ask your tax advisor for assistance in interpreting the IRS rules on this matter.

Who Pays the Costs Involved?

There will be certain expenses involved with the transfer of ownership: legal and accounting fees, appraisal and recording costs. There are no hard and fast rules as to who pays what; instead these are points to be negotiated by the donor and the institution before agreement is reached.

Remember, too, that the particular details of your agreement pertaining to a life estate or an annuity income are not automatic. If you want to receive an income from the donated property, or the right to remain in your home, you must negotiate these terms with the charitable organization before deeding the home to the institution. Your attorney and accountant must specifically structure your agreement so that it includes the benefits you wish to receive.

The Timing of Your Gift is Important

Your tax advisor can help you time your gift so that you will receive the maximum financial benefit from it, in addition to the pleasure or satisfaction you'll get from making this generous donation. Choose the year of your gift carefully. If you want to retain a life estate in your home, or if you want an annuity income from the gift property, your youth and the life expectancy tables may work against you. Your accountant may suggest that you wait a few years before deeding the property to the institution.

Another consideration is your income from other sources. You'll want to make your donation in a year when your income is high enough to be offset by the tax deduction (although some carryover is allowed).

Because charitable giving is a complicated process with an almost infinite number of variations on the theme, be sure that you seek professional legal and tax advice before you make a decision.

18

Property Tax Deferral

At a time when home values and property taxes are climbing, many older homeowners find the annual property tax bill an increasingly difficult burden to pay. Property Tax Deferral programs, available in several states and local tax jurisdictions benefit these homeowners directly by allowing them to defer the payment of their tax bill until they sell their home. Although it is an easy benefit to apply for, surprisingly few owners take advantage of it. One reason is that many older people are not aware that property tax deferral programs exist. Another reason for the low participation figures is the owners' fear that they will somehow lose their home. So the purpose of this chapter is to set the record straight and correct any misconceptions about these very useful programs.

How Property Tax Deferral Works

Property Tax Deferral programs offer government loans to homeowners for the purpose of paying their property tax bill. These loans are secured by the home and a lien against the property is recorded, just as it is for any home mortgage loan. If you move or if the property changes hands (for example, if you sell your home or die) the loan must be repaid.

A modest rate of interest is charged on your loan balance (the amount of taxes that have been deferred), but most programs do not charge application fees, appraisal fees or other loan fees.

Just as the requirements of each particular program differ, so do the registration and payment methods. It is important to know when to apply: in some areas, your application must be submitted before you pay your tax bill, while in others, you will be reimbursed if you apply after you've paid.

In some programs, your entire current property tax is paid or credited directly to your tax assessor's office. Other programs will send a check to you, that can be used only for the payment of your tax bill.

You have the option of deciding at tax time each year whether you'd like to defer that tax amount or not. For example, if your budget was tight last year and you deferred your property taxes, but this year you are able to pay them, you have the choice of paying them yourself or deferring them again. Because the deferred taxes are paid by the program in your name, the taxes are not considered delinquent. After all, you are actually paying the tax bill with **your** equity that you've built up in your home. You can never be forced to sell your home to pay the deferred taxes, nor will you be penalized in any way for choosing to take this option. The loan becomes due and payable only when you decide to move or sell your home.

How to Find Property Tax Deferral Programs

Tax deferral programs are offered by several state governments to all eligible homeowners in the state. In other states, the programs are operated by local governments; if you happen to live within that tax district, you're in luck. Taxpayers outside your district may not be as fortunate. To find out whether there is a deferral program in your area, contact the local government agency that sends you your property tax bill. If you can't locate that department, contact your state government revenue (or taxation) department. Property Tax Deferral programs are available in all or parts of the following states: (An * indicates that there is currently no statewide program available, but some local governments offer this benefit.)

California	Massachusetts*
Colorado	New Hampshire*
Connecticut*	Oregon
Florida*	Texas
Georgia	Utah
Illinois	Virginia
Iowa*	Washington
Maine	Wisconsin

Who is Eligible?

Each program varies in its eligibility requirements, so you'll want to check the specifics of the program offered in your area. First of all you must be a homeowner with a certain specified amount of equity in your home. (If you have borrowed money through large mortgages, equity loans or equity lines of credit, check to see if your level of debt will allow you to qualify.) You will not be required to have a fee appraisal of your home, but instead, the value of your equity will be determined by your property tax assessed value minus the current loan balance of your home mortgage loans.

Governments are conservative in their calculations because the loan will be repaid out of the equity in your home when you sell it. They want to be sure that there is sufficient equity to cover the loan. As a result, if you continue to defer your taxes each year at a time when housing values are not increasing, you may find that you eventually do not have sufficient equity left to continue to qualify for the tax deferral.

Most programs have a minimum age requirement (it is often 65 years, but not always). Presuming that low-to-moderate income taxpayers will have the greatest need for this benefit, most programs have an income restriction, but this varies in amount.

Advantages of Property Tax Deferral Programs

- Your property taxes are paid when they are due.

- You will not be assessed a penalty if you are unable to pay your tax bill on time.

- You put your home equity to work, by converting your equity into cash to pay property taxes.

- You will not be forced to sell or leave your home to repay the deferred taxes.

Disadvantages of Property Tax Deferral

- Not available in every community.

- Because you must have sufficient equity in your home, you may lose your eligibility later if your equity has been reduced because of deferred taxes and/or declining home value. You will not be permitted to defer additional taxes, although you do not have to repay the previously deferred taxes until you move.

- Since tax deferral takes a bite out of your home equity, you may find that your home no longer qualifies for a reverse annuity mortgage, a refinance, an equity loan or a deferred payment loan.

Part VI
A FINAL WORD

19

A Final Word

Each stage of our life brings a new set of challenges. It may not seem long at all since you were just starting adulthood and trying to figure out how to buy your first home. Or wondering how you'd ever fit baby number three into your tiny two-bedroom bungalow. No doubt, you've faced your share of real estate decisions and figure by now you've paid your dues in that department.

Don't count on it! Housing decisions keep right on coming. While those you're facing today will be quite different from the hurdles you cleared in your start-up years, they're apt to be just as challenging and worrisome as those you've dealt with in the past.

Keep this in mind: you have fifty-plus years of experience under your belt and that can certainly be a benefit when judgment calls arise, as they're bound to in housing decisions. But remember, too, that the world is moving at a mighty fast clip. We like to think that the old, traditional values remain intact but we can't ignore the fact that real estate practices, tax laws and interest rates move at mind-boggling speed. Information that was carved in stone five or ten years ago has likely been replaced by a new, improved, synthesized version that may not resemble the original at all. So our knowledge must keep pace with current events or we'll find that it's of little use to us in our everyday decisions.

That is why I wrote this book. In it, you've discovered all the up-to-date information you'll need to make wise, informed decisions about the real estate in your life. Put that together with the lifetime of experience you've acquired and the judgment you've developed, and you have what it takes to make the right move.

APPENDIX

APPENDIX I

Glossary

Adjustable-rate Mortgage Loan: Also known as an ARM loan. The lender has the right to raise or lower the interest rate at specific intervals over the life of the loan.

Amortize: To repay a loan in equal monthly payments that include both principal and interest. Most real estate loans are amortized loans.

Annuity: The payment of an agreed-upon sum of money at regular, established intervals in return for a previous deposit of money or goods. An example: an annuity may be offered to a property owner making a charitable donation of real estate.

Appraisal or Fee Appraisal: The estimated value of a property as determined by a disinterested third party, an appraiser.

Assumption: The agreement that permits a buyer to take over or assume the seller's mortgage loan obligations.

Balloon: A final lump-sum payment of the total remaining principal balance on a loan.

Basis: The value of the property at the time it was acquired. Also known as Cost Basis.

Buydown: Interest paid to the lender at the time of loan closing in exchange for a lower interest rate on the loan.

Capital Gain: The increase in value of a home or other property.

Closing: Also known as Settlement or Escrow Closing. The procedure of signing and recording the final loan and sale documents when a home is purchased or sold.

Closing Costs: Loan fees, administrative charges, recording fees and taxes paid by the buyer and seller at closing.

Contract: See Land Sales Contract.

Conventional Loan: A loan that is not insured, guaranteed or funded by a federal, state or local government. Home mortgage lenders such as banks, savings & loans, thrifts and mortgage bankers offer conventional as well as many government loans.

Counter-Offer: The seller's response (in the form of a new offer) to a buyer's offer.

Debt Service: The total amount of financing on a home. Or, a buyer's total debts.

Deed: A document signed by the seller giving the buyer title to the property.

Default: Failure to make loan payments when due.

Discount Points: Prepaid interest charged by the lender at closing, in exchange for a lower interest rate on the loan. Also known simply as Points. One point costs one percent of the loan amount.

Down Payment: The portion of the purchase price paid in cash by the buyer.

Earnest Money: A sum of money submitted by a buyer with an offer to purchase. This deposit shows the buyer's good faith and will be credited toward the purchase price at closing.

Equity: The portion of the value of the home that is owned free and clear. The value of the home minus the loan balance.

Equity Loan: A loan to a homeowner to convert a portion of the owner's equity into cash. Similar to the Equity Line of Credit, whereby an owner is able to withdraw cash as needed from an established loan fund.

Escrow officer: A neutral third party handling and recording the documents for the sale of a home. In many states, attorneys routinely carry out these functions.

Fair Market Value: The price that a willing buyer would pay a willing seller for a piece of property.

FHA: The Federal Housing Administration, a division of the U.S. Department of Housing and Urban Development, offers a government-insured loan program.

Fixed-rate Loan: A loan with an interest rate that remains the same throughout the entire term of the loan.

FmHA: The Farmers Home Administration; an agency of the federal government offering low- and moderate-income loan programs for rural areas.

FNMA (Fannie Mae), GNMA (Ginnie Mae), FHLMC (Freddie Mac): Major investors purchasing large blocks of loans at a discount from conventional and government lenders. Also known as Secondary Market Investors.

Foreclosure: Legal procedure undertaken by a lender to recover a debt after a buyer defaults.

Forward Mortgage Loan: A standard home mortgage loan, with the borrower obligated to make monthly payments to the lender. It's called a Forward Mortgage only when differentiating it from a Reverse Mortgage.

Free and Clear: Without debt; no loans against the property. As in: "They paid off their mortgage loan, so now their home free and clear."

F.S.B.O.: Pronounced "fizz-bo"; the letters stand for "For Sale By Owner" and refer to an owner who sells a home without the help of a real estate agent.

Government Loan: A loan that is funded, insured or guaranteed by a government agency.

Interest: The profit a lender receives for a loan. Usually expressed as a percentage of the loan amount.

Land Sales Contract: Also known as a Land Contract, Contract for Deed or simply Contract. An agreement between buyer and seller for the sale and seller-financing of a home or other property.

Lease Option: The lease of a home with the option to purchase it at a later date.

Life Estate: A person's legal right to hold property for the duration of their lifetime.

Loan App: Slang for Loan Application, the interview during which a loan officer gathers information from the borrower for processing the loan.

Loan Fee: Also called Loan Origination Fee. The fee charged by a lender to cover the basic cost of making a new loan. It is usually expressed as a percentage of the loan amount.

Loan-to-Value Ratio: Also called the LTV or LVR; it is the amount of the loan divided by the value of the property. It is expressed as a percentage, as in "an 80% LTV loan".

Mortgage: A document allowing the home to be used as security (collateral) for the loan. The mortgagor (borrower) gives the mortgagee (lender) a mortgage on the property.

Mortgage Insurance: An insurance policy to protect the lender against loss suffered if the buyer defaults. The buyer pays the premium. On conventional loans, it's known as PMI (Private Mortgage Insurance).

Qualify: To prove that a borrower meets a lender's financial requirements for a loan.

Prepayment Penalty: A penalty (fee) charged on some loans when the buyer pays before the due date.

Principal: The amount of money borrowed; the loan balance.

Promissory Note: Also known simply as a Note; a document in which the borrower promises to repay the loan according to the terms agreed upon.

Refinance: Also known as a Refi; a new first mortgage loan made to a homeowner, as differentiated from a Purchase Money Loan made to a homebuyer.

Reverse mortgage: A loan made to an older homeowner to convert to cash the equity he or she has acquired in the home. The lender pays the homeowner a lump sum payment or regular monthly payments which, in most cases, need not be repaid until the owner vacates the home.

Term: The length of time a borrower has to repay a standard loan.

Title: The legal right of ownership of a piece of property.

Title Insurance: Insurance issued to protect against defects in the chain of title. At closing, the seller pays for a policy to protect the buyer, while the borrower pays to protect the lender.

Trust Deed: A security document often used in place of a mortgage. Also called a Deed of Trust.

APPENDIX II
Amortization Chart

Use this chart to determine what your monthly principal and interest payment will be. Real estate loan payments are amortized over the term of the loan. That is, the payments are calculated to include the correct amount of principal and interest so that the loan balance will be zero at the end of the term.

Step 1: Find the applicable interest rate in the top row.

Step 2: Find the term of the loan in the column on the left.

Step 3: Trace down the rate column and across the term row to the square where the two meet. Remember this factor.

Step 4: Move the decimal point in your loan amount three places to the left.

Example: $57,850. becomes 57.850.

Step 5: Multiply this number by the factor found on the chart.

Example: A 10% loan with a term of 30 years would have a factor of 8.78 according to the chart. If the loan balance is $57,850, we would multiply 57.850 by 8.78 and find that our monthly payment (principal and interest) would be $507.92.

Appendix II: Amortization Chart

YEAR	8.50	8.25	8.00	7.75	7.50	7.25	7.00	6.75	6.50	6.25	6.00	5.75	5.50	5.25	5.00	4.75	4.50	4.25	4.00
1	87.22	87.10	86.99	86.87	86.76	86.64	86.53	86.41	86.30	86.18	86.07	85.95	85.84	85.72	85.61	85.49	85.38	85.26	85.15
2	45.46	45.34	45.23	45.11	45.00	44.89	44.77	44.66	44.55	44.43	44.32	44.21	44.10	43.98	43.87	43.76	43.65	43.54	43.42
3	31.57	31.45	31.34	31.22	31.11	30.99	30.88	30.76	30.65	30.54	30.42	30.31	30.20	30.08	29.97	29.86	29.75	29.64	29.52
4	24.65	24.53	24.41	24.30	24.18	24.06	23.95	23.83	23.71	23.60	23.49	23.37	23.26	23.14	23.03	22.92	22.80	22.69	22.58
5	20.52	20.40	20.28	20.16	20.04	19.92	19.80	19.68	19.57	19.45	19.33	19.22	19.10	18.99	18.87	18.76	18.64	18.53	18.42
6	17.78	17.66	17.53	17.41	17.29	17.17	17.05	16.93	16.81	16.69	16.57	16.46	16.34	16.22	16.10	15.99	15.87	15.76	15.65
7	15.84	15.71	15.59	15.46	15.34	15.22	15.09	14.97	14.85	14.73	14.61	14.49	14.37	14.25	14.13	14.02	13.90	13.78	13.67
8	14.39	14.26	14.14	14.01	13.88	13.76	13.63	13.51	13.39	13.26	13.14	13.02	12.90	12.78	12.66	12.54	12.42	12.31	12.19
9	13.28	13.15	13.02	12.89	12.76	12.63	12.51	12.38	12.25	12.13	12.01	11.88	11.76	11.64	11.52	11.40	11.28	11.16	11.04
10	12.40	12.27	12.13	12.00	11.87	11.74	11.61	11.48	11.35	11.23	11.10	10.98	10.85	10.73	10.61	10.48	10.36	10.24	10.12
11	11.69	11.55	11.42	11.28	11.15	11.02	10.88	10.75	10.62	10.49	10.37	10.24	10.11	9.99	9.86	9.74	9.62	9.50	9.38
12	11.10	10.96	10.82	10.69	10.55	10.42	10.28	10.15	10.02	9.89	9.76	9.63	9.50	9.37	9.25	9.12	9.00	8.88	8.76
13	10.61	10.47	10.33	10.19	10.05	9.92	9.78	9.65	9.51	9.38	9.25	9.12	8.99	8.86	8.73	8.60	8.48	8.35	8.23
14	10.20	10.06	9.91	9.77	9.63	9.49	9.35	9.22	9.08	8.95	8.81	8.68	8.55	8.42	8.29	8.16	8.03	7.91	7.78
15	9.85	9.70	9.56	9.41	9.27	9.13	8.99	8.85	8.71	8.57	8.44	8.30	8.17	8.04	7.91	7.78	7.65	7.52	7.40
16	9.54	9.40	9.25	9.10	8.96	8.81	8.67	8.53	8.39	8.25	8.11	7.98	7.84	7.71	7.58	7.45	7.32	7.19	7.06
17	9.28	9.13	8.98	8.83	8.69	8.54	8.40	8.25	8.11	7.97	7.83	7.69	7.56	7.42	7.29	7.15	7.02	6.89	6.76
18	9.05	8.90	8.75	8.60	8.45	8.30	8.16	8.01	7.87	7.72	7.58	7.44	7.30	7.17	7.03	6.90	6.76	6.63	6.50
19	8.85	8.70	8.55	8.39	8.24	8.09	7.94	7.79	7.65	7.50	7.36	7.22	7.08	6.94	6.80	6.67	6.53	6.40	6.27
20	8.68	8.52	8.36	8.21	8.06	7.90	7.75	7.60	7.46	7.31	7.16	7.02	6.88	6.74	6.60	6.46	6.33	6.19	6.06
21	8.52	8.36	8.20	8.05	7.89	7.74	7.58	7.43	7.28	7.14	6.99	6.84	6.70	6.56	6.42	6.28	6.14	6.01	5.87
22	8.38	8.22	8.06	7.90	7.75	7.59	7.43	7.28	7.13	6.98	6.83	6.68	6.54	6.39	6.25	6.11	5.97	5.84	5.70
23	8.26	8.10	7.93	7.77	7.61	7.46	7.30	7.14	6.99	6.84	6.69	6.54	6.39	6.25	6.10	5.96	5.82	5.68	5.55
24	8.15	7.98	7.82	7.66	7.50	7.34	7.18	7.02	6.87	6.71	6.56	6.41	6.26	6.11	5.97	5.83	5.68	5.54	5.41
25	8.05	7.88	7.72	7.55	7.39	7.23	7.07	6.91	6.75	6.60	6.44	6.29	6.14	5.99	5.85	5.70	5.56	5.42	5.28
26	7.96	7.79	7.63	7.46	7.29	7.13	6.97	6.81	6.65	6.49	6.34	6.18	6.03	5.88	5.73	5.59	5.44	5.30	5.16
27	7.88	7.71	7.54	7.37	7.21	7.04	6.88	6.72	6.56	6.40	6.24	6.08	5.93	5.78	5.63	5.48	5.34	5.19	5.05
28	7.81	7.64	7.47	7.30	7.13	6.96	6.80	6.63	6.47	6.31	6.15	5.99	5.84	5.69	5.54	5.39	5.24	5.09	4.95
29	7.75	7.57	7.40	7.23	7.06	6.89	6.72	6.56	6.39	6.23	6.07	5.91	5.76	5.60	5.45	5.30	5.15	5.00	4.86
30	7.69	7.51	7.34	7.16	6.99	6.82	6.65	6.49	6.32	6.16	6.00	5.84	5.68	5.52	5.37	5.22	5.07	4.92	4.77

Appendix II: Amortization Chart

Year	13.00	12.75	12.50	12.25	12.00	11.75	11.50	11.25	11.00	10.75	10.50	10.25	10.00	9.75	9.50	9.25	9.00	8.75
1	89.32	89.20	89.08	88.97	88.85	88.73	88.62	88.50	88.38	88.27	88.15	88.03	87.92	87.80	87.68	87.57	87.45	87.34
2	47.54	47.42	47.31	47.19	47.07	46.96	46.84	46.72	46.61	46.49	46.38	46.26	46.14	46.03	45.91	45.80	45.68	45.57
3	33.69	33.57	33.45	33.33	33.21	33.10	32.98	32.86	32.74	32.62	32.50	32.38	32.27	32.15	32.03	31.92	31.80	31.68
4	26.83	26.70	26.58	26.46	26.33	26.21	26.09	25.97	25.85	25.72	25.60	25.48	25.36	25.24	25.12	25.00	24.89	24.77
5	22.75	22.63	22.50	22.37	22.24	22.12	21.99	21.87	21.74	21.62	21.49	21.37	21.25	21.12	21.00	20.88	20.76	20.64
6	20.07	19.94	19.81	19.68	19.55	19.42	19.29	19.16	19.03	18.91	18.78	18.65	18.53	18.40	18.27	18.15	18.03	17.90
7	18.19	18.06	17.92	17.79	17.65	17.52	17.39	17.25	17.12	16.99	16.86	16.73	16.60	16.47	16.34	16.22	16.09	15.96
8	16.81	16.67	16.53	16.39	16.25	16.12	15.98	15.84	15.71	15.57	15.44	15.31	15.17	15.04	14.91	14.78	14.65	14.52
9	15.75	15.61	15.47	15.33	15.18	15.04	14.90	14.76	14.63	14.49	14.35	14.21	14.08	13.94	13.81	13.68	13.54	13.41
10	14.93	14.78	14.64	14.49	14.35	14.20	14.06	13.92	13.78	13.63	13.49	13.35	13.22	13.08	12.94	12.80	12.67	12.53
11	14.28	14.13	13.98	13.83	13.68	13.53	13.38	13.24	13.09	12.95	12.80	12.66	12.52	12.38	12.24	12.10	11.96	11.82
12	13.75	13.59	13.44	13.29	13.13	12.98	12.83	12.68	12.54	12.39	12.24	12.10	11.95	11.81	11.66	11.52	11.38	11.24
13	13.31	13.15	13.00	12.84	12.69	12.53	12.38	12.23	12.08	11.92	11.78	11.63	11.48	11.33	11.19	11.04	10.90	10.75
14	12.95	12.79	12.63	12.47	12.31	12.16	12.00	11.85	11.69	11.54	11.38	11.23	11.08	10.93	10.78	10.64	10.49	10.34
15	12.65	12.49	12.33	12.16	12.00	11.84	11.68	11.52	11.37	11.21	11.05	10.90	10.75	10.59	10.44	10.29	10.14	9.99
16	12.40	12.23	12.07	11.90	11.74	11.57	11.41	11.25	11.09	10.93	10.77	10.62	10.46	10.30	10.15	10.00	9.85	9.69
17	12.19	12.02	11.85	11.68	11.51	11.35	11.18	11.02	10.85	10.69	10.53	10.37	10.21	10.05	9.90	9.74	9.59	9.43
18	12.00	11.83	11.66	11.49	11.32	11.15	10.98	10.82	10.65	10.49	10.32	10.16	10.00	9.84	9.68	9.52	9.36	9.21
19	11.85	11.67	11.50	11.33	11.15	10.98	10.81	10.64	10.47	10.31	10.14	9.98	9.81	9.65	9.49	9.33	9.17	9.01
20	11.72	11.54	11.36	11.19	11.01	10.84	10.66	10.49	10.32	10.15	9.98	9.82	9.65	9.49	9.32	9.16	9.00	8.84
21	11.60	11.42	11.24	11.06	10.89	10.71	10.54	10.36	10.19	10.02	9.85	9.68	9.51	9.34	9.17	9.01	8.85	8.68
22	11.50	11.32	11.14	10.96	10.78	10.60	10.42	10.25	10.07	9.90	9.73	9.55	9.38	9.21	9.04	8.88	8.71	8.55
23	11.42	11.23	11.05	10.87	10.69	10.51	10.33	10.15	9.97	9.79	9.62	9.44	9.27	9.10	8.93	8.76	8.59	8.43
24	11.34	11.16	10.97	10.79	10.60	10.42	10.24	10.06	9.88	9.70	9.52	9.35	9.17	9.00	8.83	8.66	8.49	8.32
25	11.28	11.09	10.90	10.72	10.53	10.35	10.16	9.98	9.80	9.62	9.44	9.26	9.09	8.91	8.74	8.56	8.39	8.22
26	11.22	11.03	10.84	10.66	10.47	10.28	10.10	9.91	9.73	9.55	9.37	9.19	9.01	8.83	8.66	8.48	8.31	8.13
27	11.17	10.98	10.79	10.60	10.41	10.23	10.04	9.85	9.67	9.49	9.30	9.12	8.94	8.76	8.58	8.41	8.23	8.06
28	11.13	10.94	10.75	10.56	10.37	10.18	9.99	9.80	9.61	9.43	9.25	9.06	8.88	8.70	8.52	8.34	8.16	7.99
29	11.09	10.90	10.71	10.52	10.32	10.13	9.94	9.75	9.57	9.38	9.19	9.01	8.82	8.64	8.46	8.28	8.10	7.92
30	11.06	10.87	10.67	10.48	10.29	10.09	9.90	9.71	9.52	9.33	9.15	8.96	8.78	8.59	8.41	8.23	8.05	7.87

APPENDIX III

Resource List

F ree publications that you may find helpful:

American Association of Retired Persons (AARP)
Program Coordination and Development Department
Consumer Affairs
601 E Street, N.W.
Washington, DC 20049

- *Home-Made Money: Consumer's Guide to Home Equity Conversion*

  Offers detailed information about the many methods of equity conversion. Request Booklet # **D12894**

- *Your Home, Your Choice: A Workbook for older people and their families*

  Includes information about senior housing arrangements, homemaking services and other assistance, as well as continuing care communities and nursing homes. Request Booklet # **D12143**

- *Key Issues in Accessory Apartments: Zoning and Covenants Restricting Land to Residential Uses*

  What you'll need to know if you're interested in adding an apartment to a single-family home for you, your parents, your offspring or a caregiver. Request Booklet # **D1187.**

- *Key Issues in Elder Cottage Housing Opportunity (ECHO): Restrictions on Manufactured Housing*

  Restrictions relating to the use of modular housing units for senior or disabled citizens, allowing them to live close to family members or caregivers. Request Booklet # **D1186.**

- *Housing Publications List*

  For a list of other publications available from the Consumer Affairs Section of AARP, request Booklet # **D12173.**

Federal National Mortgage Association
3900 Wisconsin Ave., N.W.
Washington, D.C. 20016-2899

- *A Consumer's Guide to Senior's Housing Opportunities*

  Includes information about accessory apartments, ECHO housing, homesharing and sale-leaseback agreements.

- *Home Equity Conversion Mortgage (HECM) Information*

  This booklet describes the HUD/FHA Reverse Annuity Mortgage Programs. Request also a list of participating lenders offering reverse mortgages.

U.S.Government
Internal Revenue Service
Toll-free #: 1-800-829-3676

These publications offer detailed information about the tax laws that pertain to home ownership.

- *Tax Information for Older Americans*

  Learn all you may ever need to know about the Over-55 Capital Gains Exclusion and other tax matters affecting seniors. Request Publication # 554.

- *Tax Information for Homeowners (Including Owners of Condominiums and Cooperative Apartments)*

  Tells how to calculate your cost basis and discusses tax deductions for homeowners. Request Publication # 530.

- *Tax Information on Selling Your Home*

  More about cost basis, and what to do with all that capital gain. Request publication # 523.

And finally, not free, but well worth the dollar:

The National Center for Home Equity Conversion
1210 E College, #300
Marshall, MN 56258

- *Reverse Mortgage Locator*

Send a self-addressed stamped business-size envelope and $1.00 for a list of all the public and private sector reverse mortgage programs available in the United States.

INDEX

New Releases from
The Panoply Press Real Estate Series

First Home Buying Guide
by H.L. Kibbey
New Fourth Edition of this popular bestseller.
The complete guide for the first-time homebuyer gives a step-by-step plan for researching the market, choosing a loan, buying a home.
ISBN 0-9615067-9-2
128 pages, softcover $9.95

Appeal Your Property Taxes — and Win
by Ed Salzman
Learn what it takes to cut your tax bill. Insider's secrets from an appeals expert gives state-by-state guidelines for a winning appeal.
ISBN 1-882877-01-2
128 pages, softcover $9.95

The Growing-Older Guide to Real Estate
by H.L. Kibbey
What everyone over 50 should know about buying, selling, financing and owning a home. Equity conversion, tax considerations, buying and selling tips for stress-free real estate decisions. By the host of House Calls.
ISBN 0-9615067-8-4
192 pages, softcover $14.95

How to Finance a Home in the Pacific Northwest
by H.L. Kibbey
New Revised Edition of this award-winning book. The complete guide for financing and refinancing in Oregon and Washington state.
ISBN 1-882877-02-0
240 pages, softcover $15.95

Panoply Press books are available at bookstores everywhere. If you're unable to find any of these titles, they may be ordered by mail from the publisher, Panoply Press, Inc. Please enclose your check or money order for the cost of the books plus $3.00 shipping per order.

PANOPLY PRESS, INC.
P.O. Box 1885
Lake Oswego, OR 97035
(503) 697-7964

Printed on recycled paper